# Churchill's Secret Armies
## War Without Rules:
## Ministry of Ungentlemanly Warfare

## Ian Hall

The iconic Winston Churchill pose... defiant, confident, and proud.

# PHANTOM GAVEL PUBLICATIONS

Copyright © Ian Hall. Phantom Gavel Publications

Ian Hall is a member of the Phantom Gavel team.

ISBN-13: 978-1532793387

ISBN-10: 1532793383

# Also by Ian Hall

**Avenging Steel, a brand new Alternative History WW2 series, set in 1940's Edinburgh.**

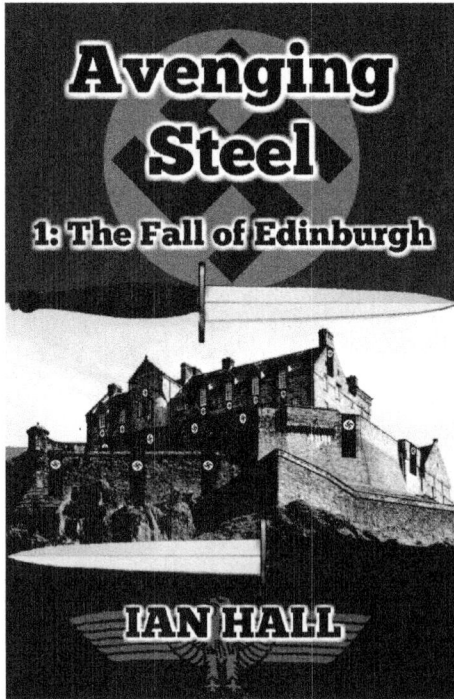

Under the noses of the new Nazi conquerors of Britain, Avenging Steel; the adventures of James Baird, philosophy student by day, S.O.E. Agent and master-spy by night….
Avenging Steel 1: The Fall of Edinburgh
Avenging Steel 2: The Nuclear Option
Avenging Steel 3: The Final Solution

# Also by Ian Hall

## World War 2 Spy School
## The Complete 1943 S.O.E.
## Counter Espionage Manual

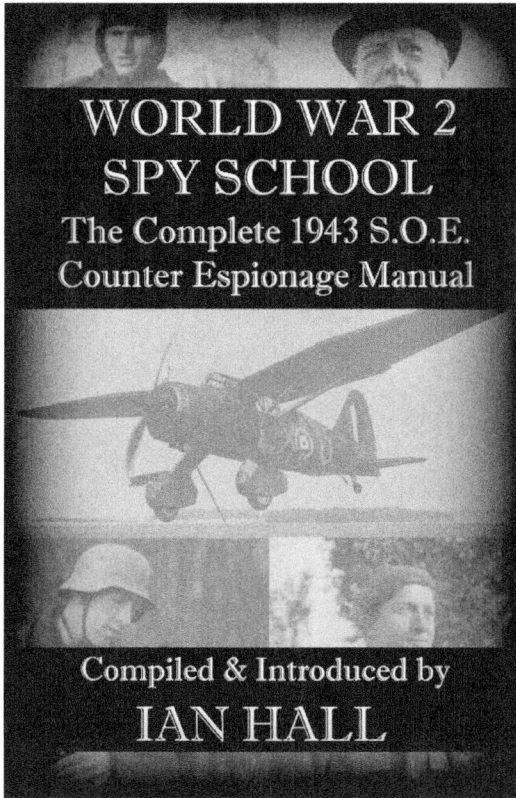

WORLD WAR 2
SPY SCHOOL
The Complete 1943 S.O.E.
Counter Espionage Manual

Compiled & Introduced by
IAN HALL

The 1943 manual used by the S.O.E. and many other Allied spy organisations in World War 2.
Copied and recreated in painstaking detail, this is the actual manual used by the instructors in training camps and bases all over the world.

And look out for the exciting new WW2 spy series;
"No Ribbons"

No Ribbons: The Road to Camp X
No Ribbons: Behind Enemy Lines


A series detailing the adventures and harrowing
actions seen by a group of S.O.E. Operatives and
their trainers.

## Dedication

This book is dedicated to those brave souls who served in Churchill's Secret Armies in World War Two. Many gained recognition in the foreign countries in which they served, yet lived secret lives 'back home'.

In writing this work, and in putting this volume to print, I pay tribute to those who fell without witness, died at the hands of the Gestapo or Japanese, or who simply vanished from the field of battle. I remember the dedication of the operatives, both covert and regular, and commend their silence in the torture chambers of the enemy and in their private lives after the war.

It is only in recent years, by the release of secret documents, that we begin to know the true story of these heroes. We live in freedom today by their devotion to duty, and their willingness to die for their mission, their people, their country, and their King.

Many of these heroes were recognized, decorated, or knighted.

But this book gives respectful praise for those who died without mention, their graves never found, their sacrifice never documented, the part they played never to be fully known or understood.

Ian Hall, 2016.

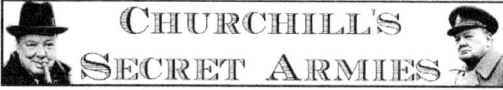

## Table of Contents

# THE DESTINY OF CHURCHILL

Research plays a huge part in the preparation of any non-fiction book, and my work for this volume is no different. It goes without saying that nuggets of the purest gold are dug up from time to time, making the whole process worthwhile, and those are coddled, emphasized and quoted by the author with relish.

In this book, I have encountered nuggets by the bucket load, all of which are presented here. It has been a complete joy to write.

However, one nugget sent a chill to my very core; a recollection by Murland de Grasse Evans, of a conversation between Winston Churchill and his then school friend.

**Churchill, aged 17, Harrow Boarding School, with classmate, George Philip**

In 1891, both boys were sixteen years old and attending Harrow School, a boarding school which Winston detested.

The nugget? It turns out that Churchill believed in destiny... his own destiny.

From his early school years he believed it was his destiny to save his country.

A rare picture, showing Winston in the full dress uniform of the 4th Hussars

When asked about his 'life's intentions', Churchill replied, the conversation going like this;

**Churchill; "I have a wonderful idea of where I shall be eventually. I have dreams about it."**

Murland; "Where is that?"

**Churchill; "I can see vast changes coming over a now peaceful world; great upheavals, terrible struggles; wars such as one cannot imagine; and I tell you London will be in danger... London will be attacked and I shall be very prominent in the defense of London."**

Murland; "How can you talk like that? We are forever safe from invasion, since the days of Napoleon."

**Churchill; "I see further ahead than you do. I see into the future. This country will be subject to a tremendous invasion, by what means I do not know, but I tell you I will be in command of the defenses of London and I shall save London and England from disaster."**

Murland; "Will you be a general then, in command of the troops?"

**Churchill; "I don't know; dreams of the future are blurred but the main objective is clear. I repeat London will be in danger, and in the high position I occupy, it will fall to me to save the capital and save the Empire."**

I'm sorry, but as I've said so many times in the writing of this book... you can't make stuff like this up!

Winston Churchill, aged 7, in 1881

# THE INTRODUCTION

This book is not a biography of Winston Churchill, or the Second World War; wiser scholars with more time on their hands have already committed themselves to that task, and presented their detailed findings far more eloquently than I ever could.

Neither was it intended to be an in-depth study of any one particular Churchill brainchild or any single 'secret army'; again such histories have already been written, and by many better informed historians than myself.

'Churchill's Secret Armies' gives a general introduction to the man himself, yes, but it is not the man himself I seek to discover. His sharp, incisive forward thinking gave rise to many innovative military units, and it is these 'secret armies', the fruits of his labor, that the book will focus upon.

Churchill chose military uniform depending on the occasion or ceremony

From the evacuation of the British Expeditionary Force at Dunkirk, just seventeen days into his Prime Minister-ship, Churchill knew he had little time, money or resources to save Britain from near-certain invasion. And yet he managed it. In just five short years, he rallied an Empire, organized a world-wide alliance, and toppled Hitler's Third Reich; the evil Realm prepared for ten years, built to last a millennia.

From the outset of the war, knowing he had little assets other than the men he commanded, he encouraged ideas in the people he gathered around him. Churchill was insightful, of that there is no doubt, but he was indeed far more. He was a revolutionary of his time, a man who seemed to come alive under stress, to thrive under times of hardship, and a man who could inspire others to greatness.

Despite Churchill's growing years, his staff in the war years would remember his boundless energy, and although his nickname "The Old Man" was commonly used, none could keep up with him. From his first breath of the day, to closing his eyes at night, he would have pen and paper close by his side. The next day's morning papers were delivered by midnight, and he read them before going to sleep. Six hours later his morning began with furious notes taken in longhand by two secretaries; Winston hated the noise of typewriters.

Winston inspecting batteries, with daughter Mary, and General Frederick Pile, around 1940

To help understand his encompassing presence, one facet of his personality must be remembered; he had an innate understanding of the broad oversight of a subject, and yet at times mired himself in details when the opportunity necessitated it. He would ask for memoranda to be prepared on "Argentina's possible entry to the war", then contemplate the effect of civilian air raid precautions in Iceland, if it ever was invaded.

Add his military acumen to this dichotomy, and you begin to build a picture of a behemoth of a man; he was capable of comprehending complex strategic overlays which overwhelmed the normal politician, and yet mused over details and innovations of his own. In 1915, as First Lord of the Admiralty, he was in personal charge of the development of the new invention of the 'tank' (then a Royal Navy directive). In 1917, he envisaged and sketched the idea of floating harbors (intended for use in Denmark), used to great effect on D-day, nearly 30 years later.

In early 1940, Churchill asked General Ismay to investigate "some projectile which can be fired from a rifle at a tank, like a rifle grenade". The first prototype was available in months. Churchill's mind simply never stopped.

Winston Churchill has been voted the 'Greatest Ever Briton' in so many polls, I wonder why the media would ever take the time to conduct another.

**Winston Churchill, around 1929**

Not all of these 'secret armies' have Churchill's brainchild stamp on them; some like Bletchley Park and RAF Fighter Command were set up some years before. But even so, Winston Churchill placed his own personal influence on everyone he met, inspiring his commanders to higher standards and pushing them to the heights he expected. He visited these centers of excellence often, mixing with both commanders and lowest workers alike.

Everyone loved Winston.

**Winston had a constitution of an ox, and the stubbornness of a mule**

When I started this book, I had envisaged a short volume of ten secret armies, maybe twelve, but it seems that even I had underestimated the genius of the man. When I reluctantly called a halt to my research, I had encountered twenty-eight, with more obscure links to many more.

Twenty-eight new, innovative ways to wage war on the enemy; some gentlemanly, some distinctly 'down-and-dirty'.

I fully realize that part of the revolution in innovation was brought on by the new modern method of war fought from 1939 to 1945. When war was first declared, many of the existing old-school generals considered this new conflict to be another trench war. The French trust in the concrete walls of the Maginot Line was a naïve fantasy, although this was thought in the 1930's to be the ultimate defense against German aggression. In 1939, facing the coming Blitzkrieg of the German

Panzer divisions, 10% of the Polish Army were cavalry and lancer battalions.

The six years of World War 2 brought more technological advances in more subjects than in any other six years of human existence. While human limits were pressed to bursting point, so too were the world's industry, its scientists and thinkers.

Polish cavalry, 1938; the 'modern' anti-tank rifle, by WW2 woefully ineffective

I have taken much care to include as many of Churchill's Secret Armies as I can find. I'm not saying my list is exhaustive nor complete, and I apologize for any which I have missed. If I have left out your pet project or your relative's unit, then take some comfort; perhaps it was just too 'secret' for me to find.

I hope you find the short history interesting, and thank you for your indulgence in my passion.

Ian Hall

Churchill (with "Tommy" gun) was genuinely interested in any weapon; he liked the hands-on approach, and often insisted on taking part at demonstrations

# THE MAN HIMSELF; WINSTON LEONARD SPENCER-CHURCHILL

Winston (right) with his mother and brother Jack. Winston was in boarding school most of his childhood

Not being considered by his father to be of 'scholarly' material, Winston Churchill attended Sandhurst Military Academy. He graduated eighth in a class of 150, and received a commission in the 4th Queens Hussars. With hindsight it is easy to see that his training in the role of wartime Prime Minister begins here, and since this is not a detailed history of Winston's life, I mention the salient points only in list form...

In 1895 he came under fire observing Spanish troops against Cuban guerrillas. It was in that short visit that he took interest in Cuban cigars, a vice for the rest of his life.

For three years he fought against native forces in India, coming under fire many times, saying; "Nothing in life is so exhilarating as to be shot at without result". He fired back, recounting his 'kills' with some considerable detachment. There is no doubt that the leader who sent his soldiers forth to kill the enemy, had already done so himself.

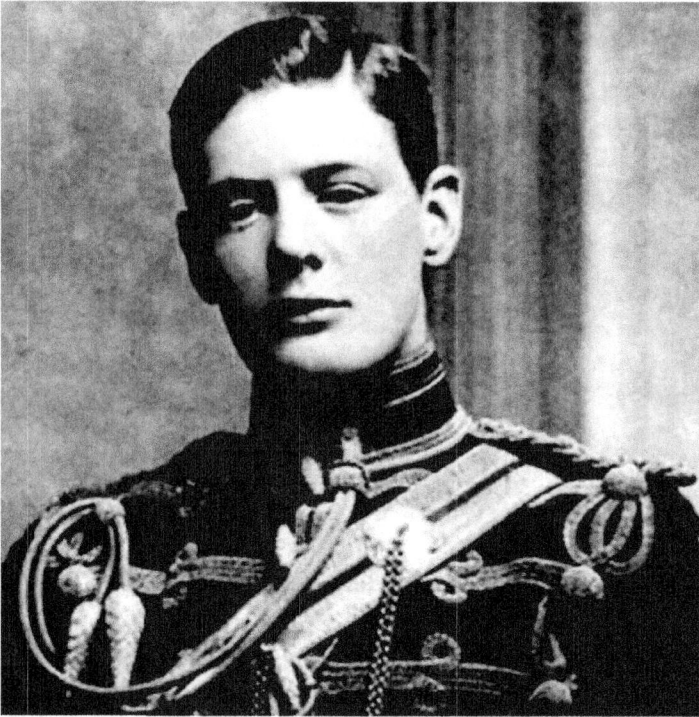
Winston Churchill, in the uniform of a Coronet of the 4th Hussars, circa 1887

In September 1898, attached to the 21$^{st}$ Lancers in Egypt, he participated in the last British cavalry charge at the Battle of Omdurman. He returned to Britain to finish a history of the Sudan Wars.

He resigned from the army in 1899, after an unsuccessful attempt as a politician, entered the Boer war as a journalist. On Nov 15$^{th}$, Churchill was captured by the Boers and placed in a POW camp. Realizing there was an opportunity for escape, he paid his debts in the camp, wrote a letter of apology to the Boer Minister of War, then scaled the wall to freedom.

Labeled by newspapers as a "modern Prince Charlie", he grabbed a ride on a passing train, and slept in ditches behind enemy lines, stealing food and clothes. Following the railway, he would read old newspapers telling of the manhunt to recapture him. He ultimately took passage on a train bound for the Portuguese colony of Delagoa Bay. He lived for weeks behind enemy lines and travelled 300 miles to safety.

The escapade made him a hero and household name in Britain, and when he returned home, he was able to launch his political career.

Churchill, in 1900, aged 26, ready for a political career

In 1900, the war hero was swiftly elected and just as quickly rose in parliamentary ranks, a true rising star in the Tory party.

In the cabinet in 1909, he oversaw the founding of the Secret Service Bureau, the very first military intelligence unit, under the Admiralty. The SSB had many departments, but would eventually develop into two sections, one becoming the Secret Intelligence Service (SIS) or Military Intelligence (MI5), and department 6 of the SSB would eventually be known simply as MI6. Churchill made certain he knew every man involved in the fledgling SSB, in both social and professional situations.

In 1915, as Lord of the Admiralty, Churchill was heavily involved with the development of the first tank. He appointed the "Landships Committee" to produce a working model.

Churchill was also the main force behind the Gallipoli campaign, which turned out to be a military disaster. He soon learned that bad intelligence had been the main factor in the defeat, and resigned from parliament in disgust at his involvement with the project. He immediately asked for a war command and he fought in the trenches in the front line in command of the 6th battalion of Royal Scots Fusiliers. In the notorious Ypres salient, it is recorded he made no less than 36 forays into no-mans-land, before returning to take up another position in parliament.

With all his experience (both good and bad) just waiting to be marshalled, he now had to impatiently wait on 'his' war to happen. Churchill's 'wilderness years' had begun. He was one of the few who consistently spoke out against the rise of Hitler's Germany, and his proliferation of armaments, a direct breaking of the Treaty of Versailles.

**A dressed-down Prime Minister Winston Churchill in 1940**

On 3 September 1939, the day Britain declared war on Germany, Churchill again took up his appointment as First Lord of the Admiralty. Holding such office, he was a member of Chamberlain's small War Cabinet. He proved to be one of the highest-profile ministers during the first few months when the only real fighting was in Poland and eastern Europe. With his typical forward thinking, Churchill called for occupation of the neutral Norwegian iron-ore port of Narvik and the iron mines in Kiruna, Sweden. Such a seizure would be a terrible blow to Germany's source of iron ore, and thus the German war effort. Prime

Minister Chamberlain disagreed, and the operation was delayed until after the successful German invasion of Norway, a tactical misstep.

By May 1940, it became clear that, following failure in Norway, the country had no confidence in Prime Minister Chamberlain's prosecution of the war and Chamberlain resigned.

Churchill came to power as Prime Minister on 10th May, 1940 on the very same day that Germany attacked British, Belgian, Dutch and French forces.

The phrase *'commeth the hour, commeth the man'* would never be more poignant than that moment.

Malvolio in Shakespeare's *Twelfth Night*, said; *'Be not afraid of greatness. Some are born great, some achieve greatness, and others have greatness thrust upon them.'*

Whatever sentiment you chose, the hour had chosen the man; Winston Churchill, the only leader who had the experience, foresight and forward thinking to win against Hitler.

Three days later, as his men buckled under the blitzkrieg of the German advance, Churchill gave his first address to the House of Commons;

*"...To form an administration of this scale and complexity is a serious undertaking in itself, but it must be remembered that we are in the preliminary stage of one of the greatest battles in history, that we are in action at many points in Norway and in Holland, that we have to be prepared in the Mediterranean, that the air battle is continuous and that many preparations have to made here at home. In this crisis I hope I may be pardoned if I do not address the House at any length today. I hope that any of my friends and colleagues, or former colleagues, who are affected by the political reconstruction, will make all allowance for any lack of ceremony with which it has been necessary to act. I would say to the House, as I said to those who have joined this government: "I have nothing to offer but blood, toil, tears and sweat."*

*"We have before us an ordeal of the most grievous kind. We have before us many, many long months of struggle and of suffering. You ask, What is our policy? I will say; "It is to wage war, by sea, land and air, with all our might and with all the strength that God can give us: to*

*wage war against a monstrous tyranny, never surpassed in the dark lamentable catalogue of human crime. That is our policy." You ask, What is our aim? I can answer with one word: Victory - victory at all costs, victory in spite of all terror, victory however long and hard the road may be; for without victory there is no survival."*

**On taking his place as Prime Minister, Churchill's short speech in parliament showed his determination to get on with the job**

Churchill had always been a great orator, he had toured America in the 1920's giving speeches, but in World War 2 his wordsmithing thrust to the fore. No one's speeches are remembered more than his, and many are memorized unknowingly.

But as Churchill spoke to the House, he had little idea of the overwhelming defeat his troops were facing. Less than a month later, his precious British Army would lie in tatters, their equipment scattered in France, their ability to resist an invasion temporarily gone.

# THE DIARY OF EVENTS

Announced Prime Minister on the 10th May, 1940, Winston Churchill was sixty-six years old, and exactly five months to the day away from being a grandfather for the first time. It seemed to many that he was beyond his best years. As history can attest, this was not to be the case

After the fall of France and the subsequent debacle at Dunkirk, Churchill, with his back to the wall, worked like a man possessed. With invasion apparently staring him in the face, he used every minute in every day to improve the lot of his country. He encouraged every idea that came into the minds of his aides must be spoken out loud. He dismissed hundreds, but as we shall see in the list of his 'secret armies', he acceded to many of them.

In the first days of June, 1940, Churchill issued so many clandestine orders that his aides could hardly keep up. If we look at the inception dates for his secret armies, we see how quickly after the fall of Dunkirk he took command of the situation.

Winston Churchill, inspecting Air Raid Precaution (ARP) wardens in Coventry

Here's an overview in diary form...

September 4th 1939, **Bletchley Park, or Station 'X'**. The day after the UK declared war on Germany, Turing reported to Bletchley Park.

April 20th 1940, **Independent Companies** formed. Raised quickly for commando attacks in Norway, these units would soon be 're-branded' as Commandoes.

May 10th, 1940, **Winston Churchill** made Prime Minister of Britain.

May 27th 1940, **The Little Boats, Operation Dynamo**; the organization behind the evacuation of Dunkirk.

June 4th 1940, the **British Expeditionary Force (BEF);** the last of the men are rescued from Dunkirk.

June, 1940, **Auxiliary Units** initiated. These groups would rise to commit sabotage after the imminent German invasion.

June, 1940, **Special Duty Branch**, set up by SIS to monitor the public for loose talk and dangerous information.

June 13th 1940, **Special Operations Executive (SOE)** set up, bringing three separate intelligence organisations under one command.

June 20th 1940, **British Security Coordination** set up in New York. (To coordinate espionage and propaganda work in the western hemisphere)

June, 1940, **Long Range Desert Group** formed; the pre-cursor to the SAS. (To strike behind enemy lines in the north African theatre)

June, 1940, **Commandoes** formed, taking men from the previously named Independent Companies. (To strike in mainland Europe)

July 1st, 1940, the **Bureau Central de Renseignements et d'Action (BCRA)** The Free French government-in-exile formed its own intelligence unit, following the British SOE model.

Churchill with wife, Clementine, and daughter, Mary. Despite his harrowing war work, Churchill also had a huge public appearance diary

July 1940, the **Special Boat Section (SBS)** formed. This navy-based special operations unit would be the fore-runner of all navy Seals.

July, 1940, **Special Service Brigade** formed.

July 10th, 1940**, Battle of Britain's Fighter Command**. No collection of Churchill's Secret Armies would be complete without a mention of the pilots, ground crew, and support staff of Britain's Royal Air Force.

17th July, 1940, the **Combined Operations Headquarters** was set up as an overseer of combined forces attacks on continental Europe.

September 20th, 1940, the **Cichociemni (Silent Unseen)** were formed. Basically they were elite special-ops paratroopers of the Polish Army, SOE trained, sent back behind enemy lines.

October 1940, his first grandchild, Winston, is born.

November 1940, **Commandos** commence parachute training at Ringway airfield, near Manchester.

March 1941, **Norwegian Independent Company 1** raised by Special Operations Executive (SOE) originally for the purpose of performing commando raids during the occupation of Norway by Nazi Germany.

He frequently inspected all varieties of troops under his command. In those dark times, his visits were warmly welcomed, and a great morale boost

March 1941, the creation of **Advanced Headquarters 'A' Force** ('A' Force) in Cairo, under the command of Brigadier Dudley Clarke. This department was the very beginning of Deception as a weapon in war.

July, 1941, the official **Special Air Service (SAS)** was formed.

Aug 1941, the **Political Welfare Executive** was formed, charged with political propaganda, formed from SOI, the propaganda wing of the SOE.

Sept 1941, **London Controlling Section** formed to coordinate Allied military deception, taking the 'deception' work of 'A' Force to other theaters of war. Formed Ops (B) in 1943.

Dec 1941, **Military Intelligence Dept 9 (MI9),** long under the powerful boot of MI6, SOE, and PWE, MI9 becomes its own organization, with separate personnel, offices and budget. Responsible to help get aid to POW's in camps and assist escaped POW's to reach home soil.

January 1942, the very beginnings of **Operation Pluto**. The plan to provide D-Day with a fuel pipeline for use on the French coast.

1942, the **Royal Air Force Commandos** formed 15 commando units in 1942, each 150 strong. These units contained technicians and armourers to allow the forward operation of friendly fighters by servicing and arming them from captured air fields.

Feb, 1942, the **No. 161 (Special Duties) Squadron** was formed to provide specialist transport for SOE agents in Europe.

March 1942, **Z Special Unit** created. Basically it was the SOE of the Australian campaign against the Japanese.

May, 1942, **the Mulberry Harbor**; Winston Churchill issued a memo 'Piers for use on beaches', resulting in the development of the floating Mulberry Harbor.

Sept 1942**, 30 Assault Unit** formed. A Special Forces unit, (formed by Louis Mountbatten and Ian Fleming), usually sent or parachuted ahead of conventional forces to capture personnel or information.

Late 1942, the **Royal Naval Commandos** were raised. By the end of the war, 22 companies existed to establish, maintain and control beachheads during amphibious operations.

1943, **Hobart's Funnies**. Despite their odd name, these innovative tank adaptions saved lives on D-Day.

October 1943, the **712th Survey Flotilla** was created. This intrepid group of hydrographers, had the dangerous task of surveying the possible landing sites for D-Day.

June 1944, **Operation Jedburgh**. A combined SOE/OSS/BCRA operation to encourage resistance behind enemy lines during and after D-Day.

Churchill's 'V for Victory' sign became an enduring iconic image. If he forgot to do it, people in the crowd would shout for it

# THE SPEECHES OF WINSTON CHURCHILL

In April 1963, President John F. Kennedy, when making Winston Churchill an Honorary Citizen of the United States of America said; "He mobilized the English language, and sent it into battle".

If it is sufficiently important for President Kennedy to mention the strength and bravery of Churchill's words, then I feel it is imperative that I also do so. Churchill's oratory skills are probably as important as any one of his physical 'secret armies'. No leader of the time is quoted more, none remembered more.

From 1940 to 1945 and beyond he encouraged the troops and civilians alike to keep the struggle going, and 'never surrender'. His speeches encouraged other countries and other world leaders to join Britain in its 'hour of need', making his words an important part of his military arsenal.

His incisive wit is also remembered, and I make no apologies in also including them.

I list some of the more prominent speeches, in very rough date order.

**Winston Churchill and Lady Nancy Astor, long-term combatants in Parliament**

## CHURCHILL TO NANCY ASTOR
## 1912, BLENHEIM PALACE

Nancy Astor: "If I were married to you, I'd put poison in your coffee."

Churchill: "If I were married to you, I'd drink it."

## ALSO TO LADY ASTOR,

Lady Astor: "You're drunk, Winston, and what's more you're disgustingly drunk."

Churchill: "My dear, you are ugly, and what's more, you are disgustingly ugly. But tomorrow I shall be sober and you will still be disgustingly ugly."

## A LONE VOICE QUESTIONING APPEASEMENT TO HITLER
## BROADCAST, LONDON, 16 NOVEMBER, 1934.

At present we lie within a few minutes' striking distance of the French, Dutch and Belgian coasts, and within a few hours of the great aerodromes of Central Europe. We are even within canon-shot of the Continent.

So close as that! Is it prudent, is it possible, however much we might desire it, **to turn our backs upon Europe** and ignore whatever may happen there? I have come to the conclusion – reluctantly I admit – **that we cannot get away**. Here we are and we must make the best of it. But do not underrate the risks – the grievous risks – we have to run.

## ON CHAMBERLAIN'S RETURN "PEACE IN OUR TIME"
## HOUSE OF COMMONS, 5 OCTOBER 1938

This is only the beginning of the reckoning. This is only the first sip, the **first foretaste of a bitter cup** which will be proffered to us year by year unless, by a supreme recovery of moral health and martial vigor, we arise again and take our stand for freedom as in the olden time.

## BLOOD, TOIL, TEARS AND SWEAT
## THE HOUSE OF COMMONS, MAY 13, 1940

I would say to the House, as I said to those who have joined this Government: **I have nothing to offer but blood, toil, tears and sweat.** We have before us an ordeal of the most grievous kind. We have before us many, many long months of struggle and of suffering. You ask, what is our policy? I can say: It is to wage war, by sea, land and air, with all our might and with all the strength that God can give us; to **wage war against a monstrous tyranny**, never surpassed in the dark, lamentable catalogue of human crime. This is our policy. You ask, what is our aim? I can answer in one word: It is victory, victory at all costs, victory in spite of all terror, victory, however long and hard the road may be, **for without victory, there is no survival**.

"Nothing to offer but blood, toil, tears and sweat"

### THE RETREAT FROM FLANDERS
### BEFORE THE HOUSE OF COMMONS, JUNE 4, 1940

Even though large tracts of Europe and many old and famous states have fallen or may fall into the grip of the Gestapo and all the odious apparatus of Nazi rule, we shall not flag or fail. We shall go on to the end, we shall fight in France, we shall fight on the seas and oceans, **we shall fight with growing confidence and growing strength in the air**, we shall defend our island, whatever the cost may be, we shall fight on the beaches, we shall fight on the landing grounds, we shall fight in the fields and in the streets, we shall fight in the hills; **We shall never surrender** and even if, which I do not for the moment believe, this island or a large part of it were subjugated and starving, then our empire beyond the seas, armed and guarded by the British Fleet, will carry on the struggle until in God's good time the New World with all its power and might, sets forth to the liberation and rescue of the Old.

We must be careful not to assign to this deliverance the attributes of a victory. **Wars are not won by evacuations.**

Soldiers (possibly Home Guard) stand triumphant beside a downed Messerschmitt ME-109. Intact specimens, such as this one, were studied in great detail

### ANTICIPATING THE BATTLE OF BRITAIN
### BEFORE THE HOUSE OF COMMONS, JUNE 18, 1940

What General Weygand called the Battle of France is over. I expect that **the Battle of Britain is about to begin.** Upon this battle depends the survival of Christian civilization. upon it depends our own British life and the long continuity of our institutions and our Empire. The whole fury and might of the enemy must very soon be turned on us now. Hitler knows that he will have to break us in this island or lose the war. If we can stand up to him, all Europe may be free and the life of the world may move forward into broad, sunlit uplands. But if we fail, then the whole world, including the United States, including all that we have known and cared for, **will sink into the abyss of a new Dark Age**, made more sinister, and perhaps more **protracted, by the lights of perverted science.** Let us therefore brace ourselves to our duties, and so bear ourselves that, **if the British Empire and its Commonwealth last for a thousand years, men will say, "This was their finest hour."**

## WINNING THE BATTLE OF BRITAIN
## HOUSE OF COMMONS, 20 AUGUST, 1940

The gratitude of every home in our Island, in our Empire, and indeed throughout the world, except in the abodes of the guilty, goes out to the British airmen who, undaunted by odds, unwearied in their constant challenge and mortal danger, are turning the tide of the World War by their prowess and by their devotion. **Never before in the field of human conflict was so much owed by so many to so few.**

## CHURCHILL, ON THE TOILET IN THE HOUSE OF COMMONS,

Secretary (after knocking on the door): "Excuse me Prime Minister, but the Lord Privy Seal wishes to speak to you."

Churchill: "Tell His Lordship: I'm sealed on The Privy and can only deal with one shit at a time"

Churchill addressing Congress, Dec 26th, 1941

## ASKING FOR AMERICAN AID
## 9 February, 1941

President Roosevelt. Put your confidence in us - give us your faith and your blessing and under Providence all will be well. We shall not fail or falter, we shall not weaken or tire - neither the sudden shock of

37

battle nor the long drawn trails of vigilance or exertion will wear us down. **Give us the tools and we will finish the job.**

### CHURCHILL, SPEECH TO CONGRESS
### 26 DECEMBER 1941

Hope has returned to the hearts of scores of millions of men and women, and with **that hope there burns the flame of anger against the brutal, corrupt invader** ... In a dozen famous ancient States now prostrate under the Nazi yoke, the masses of the people ... await the hour of liberation ... That hour will strike, and its solemn peal will proclaim that **the night is past and that the dawn has come.**

### LORD MAYOR'S LUNCHEON, LONDON,
### 10 NOVEMBER 1942

...this is not the end. It is not even the beginning of the end. But it is perhaps **the end of the beginning.**

### SINEWS OF PEACE
### WESTMINSTER COLLEGE, FULTON, MISSOURI MARCH, 5, 1946

From Stettin in the Baltic to Trieste in the Adriatic, **an iron curtain** has descended across the Continent.

### HYDE PARK GATE, LONDON,
### 30 NOVEMBER 1949

Photographer: "I hope, sir, that I will shoot your picture on your hundredth birthday."

Churchill: "I don't see why not, young man. You look reasonably fit and healthy."

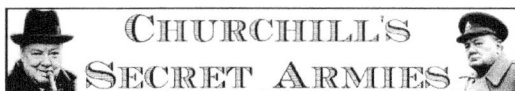

# THE KEY PERSONNEL

Winston Churchill had many attributes which made him the perfect man to be in charge at the time. One of these was the natural ability to surround himself with key personnel. The experiences and ideas of these men and women were essential in the creation of Churchill's Secret Armies.

**Hugh Dalton**; as cabinet minister, he was Minister of Economic Warfare from 1940–42. He helped establish the Special Operations Executive (SOE), and was a member of the executive committee of the Political Warfare Executive (PWE).

Sir Colin McVean Gubbins, used three times in Churchill's Secret Armies

**Colin Gubbins**; an officer much used by Churchill. Firstly, in command of the Independent companies, the precursor to the Commandoes, then heading the Auxiliary Units, and eventually as boss of the Special Operations Executive (SOE).

**Peter Wilkinson**; an ever-present aide of Colin Gubbins. Not only did he work under Gubbins in the Auxiliary Units and SOE, he also flew missions into Slovenia and Austria.

**Dudley Clarke**; A pioneer of military deception and founder of the London Controlling Section, he was also instrumental in the origination of the British Commandos, the Special Air Service and the US Rangers. It was Dudley Clarke who first suggested the name 'Rangers' to Wild Bill Donovan.

**Peter Fleming**; The originator of the Auxiliary Units, and head of 'D' division, in charge of London Controlling Section (LCS) military deceptions, Far East. He was brother of SEO member and James Bond author, Ian Fleming.

**William Stephenson**; as head of the British Security Coordination, in New York, Stephenson was responsible almost single-handedly changing American public opinion to joining the war with Germany. He worked with both Roosevelt and Donovan to advance his message.

**David Stirling**; originally Scots guards, he joined the commandoes, the Z-force. Convinced of the strength of small assault groups, he dreamed up a new force; the SAS.

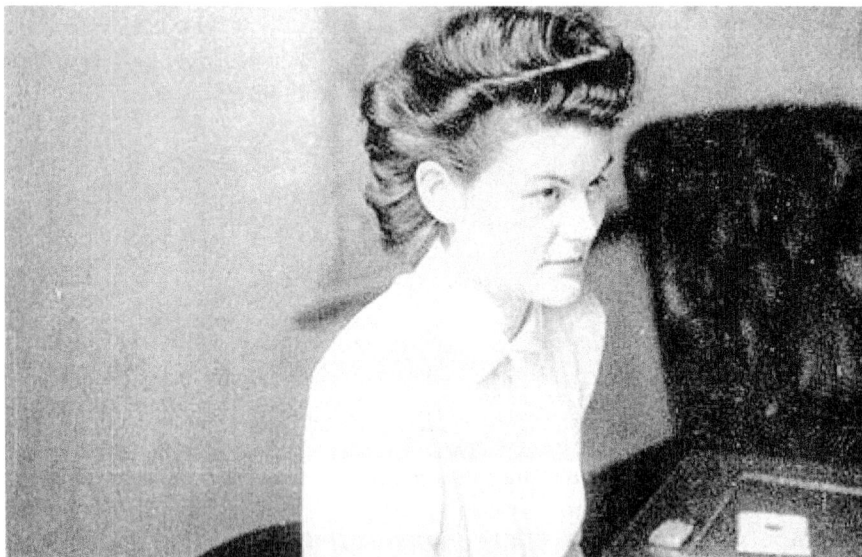

Joan Bright Astley, present in every intelligence meeting with Churchill

**Joan Bright Astley**; worked in various Intelligence departments in Churchill's War cabinet, dated Ian Fleming, and was one of the women on whom he modelled 'Moneypenny'. She was present in every one of Churchill's intelligence meetings.

Ian Fleming in 1962, with Sean Connery on the set of Dr No. Fleming got to see three of his books made into films before he died, aged just 56

**Ian Fleming**; originally worked as Admiral Godfrey's personal assistant and as a liaison with the Secret Intelligence Service, the Political Warfare Executive, the Special Operations Executive (SOE), and the Joint Intelligence Committee. He helped Donovan devise the OSS, and was involved directly in command of several commando squadrons, including 30 Assault Group and T-Force.

**John Bevan**; worked for MI5, then the Norwegian campaign. Later with Dudley Clarke, set up the London Controlling Section (LCS), rising to controlling officer. He was responsible for Operation Mincemeat's delivery to Churchill. Involved in Operation Bodyguard at D-day. Responsible for the idea of Ops (B), a deception dept responsible to Eisenhower.

**Ronald Wingate**; the 2IC of the London Controlling Section, under John Bevan. Together they devised Operation Mincemeat, and the deception of Operation Bodyguard.

**James Michael Calvert**; 'Mad Mike' commanded Commandoes in Norway, then moved to the far east. He worked with the Chindits and in

41

guerilla actions in the jungle. Always leading from the front, he led many operations against the Japanese.

Dennis Wheatley, famous spy novelist; for Churchill he wore his cloak and dagger for real

**Dennis Wheatley**; already a famous novelist before the war, Wheatley was drafted into Churchill's inner intelligence sanctum. Initially he offered planning assistance, later placed in the LCS (deception) with Bevan and Clarke.

# THE MILITARY INTELLIGENCE DEPARTMENTS

The **Secret Service Bureau (SSB)** was formed in 1909, under close scrutiny by Winston Churchill. The bureau was immediately split into naval and army sections, and as the Great War approached, again into other departments which specialized in domestic issues, espionage and various others.

Department designation was formalized before the outbreak of the Great War in 1914. Soon the list Directorate of Military Intelligence became solidified.

Included here for your clarity later is the list of British Military Intelligence Departments, first formed in 1909 and divided/fragmented over the next nine years to 1918. So many of World War 2 intelligence departments took inspiration or indeed their beginnings from this list, I thought it proper to include it at the beginning, well, relatively at the beginning.

Incidentally, if any MI numbers have been omitted from the list... they simply don't exist.

(Maybe it's the beginning of the end, or to quote Churchill, maybe it's just "the end of the beginning".)

| Designation | Activities |
| --- | --- |
| MI1 | Department of Codes and cyphers. Later merged with other code-breaking agencies. These became the core of the Government Code and Cypher School (GCCS; now known as the Government Communications Headquarters (GCHQ)) first started in 1938 at Bletchley Park. |
| MI2 | Department of Middle Eastern Studies; including Middle and Far East. At times this came to include Scandinavia, US, USSR, Central and South America. |
| MI3 | Department of Eastern Europe and the Baltic Provinces (plus USSR, Eastern Europe and Scandinavia after Summer 1941). |
| MI4 | Geographical section—maps (transferred to Military Operations in April 1940). |

MI5                    British home counter-intelligence.

The official insignia of MI5

MI6                    Liaison with Secret Intelligence Service (SIS) and the Foreign Office.

MI7                    Department of Press and Propaganda. Transferred to Ministry of Information in May 1940.

MI8                    Signals interception and communications security.

MI9                    Escaped British PoW debriefing, escape and evasion. PoW escape tactics and assistance (also: enemy PoW interrogation until 1941).

The crest of MI6

MI10                   Technical Intelligence worldwide.

MI11             Military Security.

MI12             Liaison with censorship organisations in Ministry of Information, military censorship.

MI14             Department of German studies and German-occupied territories (Also German aerial photography until Spring 1943).

**WW2 was the first major conflict that great use was made of Arial photography**

MI15             Department of Aerial photography. In the Spring of 1943, aerial photography moved to the Air Ministry and MI15 became air defense intelligence.

MI16             Scientific Intelligence (formed in 1945).

MI17             Secretariat for Director of Military Intelligence from April 1943.

MI19             Enemy prisoner of war (POW) interrogation. (From MI9 in Dec 1941)

MI (JIS)             Related to Joint Intelligence Staff, a sub-group of the Joint Intelligence Committee. Axis planning staff.

MI L(R)             Russian Liaison.

Prisoner of war interrogation; never a dinner topic, but necessary in time of war

# THE SETTING OF THE SCENE

On 1st September, 1939, Germany invaded Poland.

The Polish Army had a million men waiting on the attack, but what they did not find themselves prepared for was the speed on which it was delivered. Twenty-seven days later Poland surrendered.

The world had been introduced to the concept of modern warfare.

Heinz Guderian's book "Achtung Panzer" (translated literally as 'Beware; Tanks!'), published in 1937, influenced Adolf Hitler greatly. It argues for the swift use of tanks and other armored vehicles in a swift, more aggressive war than had previously been thought possible. The book focuses on the historical norm of static or 'trench warfare' during the Great War, and the development of the first tanks by Britain in 1915. Guderian also advocated the use of motorized infantry to keep up with the forward line of armor.

German Mk III, Poland, 1939; Allies 4th biggest army, Poland fell in 28 days

In the Great War, tanks had a 'high' speed of 3.7 miles per hour, a fast walking pace, and their use in offensive maneuvers were as a sideline, a support for the masses of infantry used.

By 1939, Hitler's new tanks could achieve 25 mph, a fast and formidable foe when used in large numbers. The modern French and British tanks were slower, heavier and outgunned. Elsewhere in Europe, the tanks were far more primitive.

Nazi Germany invaded Poland on 1st September 1939, marking the start of the Second World War. Immediately the British Expeditionary Force (BEF) was sent across the channel to assist in the defense of France, Hitler's obvious next target, landing at Saint Nazaire, Nantes and Cherbourg. As the allies built up their vast army in the north of France, a time of relative peace descended on Europe, called the 'phoney war'.

By May 1940, the BEF consisted of 10 divisions, under General John Vereker, situated across northern France, near the Belgian border, and were supported by the Belgian Army, and three Army Groups of the French Army.

Two million French troops awaited Hitler's attack. Bolstered by over 400,000 British, and approximately 200,000 Belgians, it was a formidable force. At the time of the first German attack, it seemed inconceivable that France would fall in a month.

British Vickers Mk VI; in armament, speed and armor, no match for German tanks

On the 251st day of the war, after many months of inaction, on 10 May 1940, Germany began a two pronged attack into France and the Low Countries. Army Group B, under Generaloberst Von Brock invaded Belgium and the Netherlands, where they were met by the whole of the

BEF. Meanwhile three Panzer corps of Army Group A under Rundstedt swung around to the south and drove for the Channel through the deeply wooded areas of the Ardennes, an area thought by the French Command too dense to lead an army through.

Although the BEF held their positions along the river Dyle in Belgium, the Belgian and French positions on their flanks failed to hold their position, forcing the British to make a withdrawal to the Escaut River on 14th May. The French Commanders had by now committed their reserves into the fight, meaning there were no French forces situated between the actual fighting and Paris; thankfully the Germans did not know this. However, this meant a clear path for Rundstedt and his tanks, the panzer and motorized infantry units rapidly drove in a flanking maneuver reaching the English Channel with incredible speed. Eleven days into the war, on 21st May, the German forces had trapped the BEF, remnants of the Belgian Army, and the three French Army Groups in an area along the northern coast of France.

General Vereker, his troops fighting a collapsing defense, immediately saw that evacuation across the Channel was the best course of action and began a withdrawal to Dunkirk, the closest location with good port facilities. Elements were changing so fast, it was difficult for any type of organization to be put in place, and soon tens of thousands of British, Belgian and French troops began to arrive on the French coastline.

**Dunkirk, May 1940; Allied troops wait patiently on the beach to be dis-embarked. Over 150,000 men were taken directly from the beaches**

49

On 22 May 1940, the allies got their first life-line. Adolf Hitler approved a halt to the German offensive, a pause to collect their own disorganization; they had simply advanced so fast, they had overstretched their supply lines. 22$^{nd}$ May 1940, turned out to be one of those crucial moments in history; if the Germans had simply pushed to the sea, the Second World War would have ended there and then. Only one battalion of the BEF was in place to stop the whole German Army seizing the port facilities and capturing half a million Allied prisoners.

Littered beaches near Dunkirk. The BEF left most of their equipment in France

But the German halt order gave the trapped Allied forces time to dig in. Using this opportunity to re-group, they fell back en-masse towards Dunkirk, congregating in a seven mile wide bubble, to await transport over the channel. The war in Europe was effectively over.

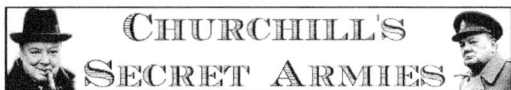

# THE MEN AND WOMEN OF BLETCHLEY PARK

### THE BLETCHLEY PARK MANSION

Although not officially one of Churchill's Secret Armies, I feel it necessary to include a short mention of Bletchley Park in my collection. Churchill praised the efforts of his codebreakers as much as he could, visited the site frequently, and held the status of intelligence highly, describing Bletchley as "the goose that laid the golden egg... but never cackled".

**Bletchley Park House; soon over 9000 people would work in the compound**

Bletchley Park was a country house purchased in May 1938 by Admiral Sir Hugh Sinclair, head of the Secret Intelligence Service (SIS or MI6). The mansion and the surrounding 58 acres were intended for use by Government Code and Cypher School (GC&CS) and SIS in the event of the war that many predicted was imminent.

(Incidentally, the GC&CS was known by the workers as the 'Golf, Cheese & Chess Society')

Bletchley Park was not only 'safe' outside London; it was situated near the intersection between the railway lines from Oxford and

Cambridge, the top two Universities where many of Bletchley's code-breakers were recruited.

When the war broke out, many on part-time contracts with GC&CS, like Alan Turing, reported for work immediately. In the first months of the war, Bletchley had humble minimalist beginnings, initially around 100 staff lived in the mansion's ground floor rooms, while the upper floors were owned and staffed by MI6. The solitary lifestyle would not continue long, by the summer of 1945, just six years later, over 9000 people worked at Bletchley Park.

Primitive conditions for intellectuals to break codes, but it worked, and the staff stayed silent for many years

Everyone who worked at the facility had to have their Bletchley Park ID's, and had signed the Official Secrets Act. Even couples who met and married at Bletchley, never talked to each other about their war work for many, many years. Some would go to their graves without once even suggesting they worked there.

Once the mansion had become full, they spilled to the garage, then the stable yard, then over 20 wooden 'huts' were built, and 8 brick-built 'blocks', eventually housing the thousands of analysts, mathematicians, crypto analysts, and scientists that staffed the compound. Security was paramount, and to this date, no leaks have been recorded from the premises. Personnel inside the compound were encouraged not to talk to fellow workers... loose lips in Bletchley Park could indeed have sunk ships.

Apart from the main mansion, here are the hut designations...

Hut 1: The first hut, built in 1939, initially housed the Wireless Station. Later it was given over to administrative functions.

Hut 2: A recreational hut (café) for "beer, tea, and relaxation".

Hut 3: General Military Intelligence. Translation, analysis of Army and Air Force decrypts.

Hut 4: Naval Military Intelligence. Analysis of German Naval Enigma and Swedish Hagelin decrypts.

Hut 5: Military Intelligence. Italian, Spanish, Portuguese ciphers and German police codes.

Hut 6: Enigma Cryptanalysis. Wehrmacht and Luftwaffe Enigma. (Gordon Welshman's hut)

Hut 7: Cryptanalysis of Japanese naval codes and intelligence.

Hut 8: Enigma Naval Cryptanalysis of Naval Enigma (Alan Turing's hut).

Hut 9: ISOS (Intelligence Section Oliver Strachey section). Oliver Strachey broke many codes during the war, and involved with the 'Double Cross System'.

Hut 10: Secret Intelligence Service (SIS or MI6) codes, Air and Meteorological sections.

Hut 11: Bombe building.

Hut 14: Communications Center.

Hut 15: SIXTA (Signals Intelligence and Traffic Analysis).

Hut 16: ISK (Intelligence Service Knox) Abwehr ciphers.

Hut 18: ISOS (Intelligence Section Oliver Strachey).

The brick-built 'block' buildings were...

Block A: Naval Intelligence.

Block B: Italian Air and Naval, and Japanese code breaking.

Block C: Stored the substantial punch-card index.

Block D: Enigma work, extending that in huts 3, 6, and 8.

Block E: Incoming and outgoing Radio Transmission and TypeX.

Block F: Included the Newmanry and Testery, and Japanese Military Air Section.

Block G: Traffic analysis and deception operations.

Block H: Tunny and Colossus.

An Enigma machine; a box of cogs, dials, and a maze of intricate wiring

## THE ENIGMA MACHINE

The first Enigma machine was developed in 1918 by German engineer Arthur Scherbius and intended to transmit discrete information in commercial and banking applications. Never a commercial success, these were taken over by the German Navy (Kriegsmarine) in 1928 as their main cypher for their 'secret' messages.

Following the navy's involvement, the German intelligence network used Enigma machines from its inception, and by 1939, the Germans believed that with Enigma they had a foolproof system of communication. They had calculated, correctly that the chances of decrypting the Enigma machine was 150, million, million, million to one.

Unfortunately, Polish cryptographers had produced their own working model of the same model used by the Germans; they passed it to Britain in September 1939. It was the beginning of their end. By design, the machine had a system... Bletchley Park's job was to work out exactly what the system was.

Alan Turing, the man who cracked the enigma code, and shortened the war

## Alan Turing

Much has already been told of Alan Turing, brilliant mathematician, computer inventor, and homosexual. Portrayed in the media in so many different ways, Turing was the historical 'star' of Bletchley Park, but in effect, many thousands of men and women labored over computer punch cards, crypto analysis, and cyphers.

The Germans changed the Enigma settings at midnight every day. Knowing that personal decryption would always be too slow to give the Allies actionable results, Turing developed a machine to read a 'computer card' system. Much is made of the computer's breaking of the code, and this is the case, but much initial decryption was done by many cryptologists to get the 'machine' into a development stage.

Every night, just after 12.00 midnight, the Bletchley park 'boffins' would spring into action, trying to break the next day's code.

One night, it did.

*'Today's the day, minus three...'* from the Italian Navy was the first message to be decoded by Bletchley Park in time to be acted upon. The Italian Navy was gathering to attack a British convoy in the Mediterranean at midnight. The problem was... how could the British act on the information without making it perfectly obvious that they had broken the code?

Rallying a plethora of spies in Cairo to hopefully disguise the origin of the message, the Royal Navy sailed anyway, dealing a vital victory against the Italian Fleet at Matapan on 27th - 29th March, 1941. The Italians lost 3 heavy cruisers, 2 destroyers, and their pride and joy, the battleship *Vittorio Veneto* was badly damaged; that one engagement ended the threat of the Italian fleet for the remainder of the war.

Once broken, the coded messages flashed through Bletchley Park like wildfire. But the victory was short-lived... for an unknown reason, the Germans changed their coding; for a while Bletchley Park was back to square one.

But not for long. Once the code had been initially broken, every subsequent attempt took less and less time. Alan Turing set his sights on decrypting the German Naval codes, to disrupt the U-Boats sinking allied shipping in the Atlantic.

By the end of the war, Bletchley Park was deciphering thousands of messages per day, making it one of Britain's most potent weapons.

Colossus; the computing machine that broke the Enigma and Lorenz codes

## COLOSSUS

There is one story that got lost a little in the general history of Bletchley Park, and yet was just as important as the Enigma codes.

In 1940, Hitler decided that he wanted his own private encryption machine; a machine that Hitler and Hitler's High Command used; the system known as LORENZ.

**Bill Tutte,** using only statistical mathematics took to the task, resurfacing four months later with a solution to break the Lorenz code.

Considering the allies did not actually have a physical Lorenz machine, it was nothing short of brilliant. One writer, who examined the theory thirty years later, described Tutte's work as 'one of the greatest intellectual feats of World War Two'.

**Tommy Flowers** (a friend of Alan Turing) working at the Pot Office, was drafted to Bletchley park, where he designed the first semi programmable electronic computer, calling it Colossus because of its immense size.

The actual machine parts for Colossus arrived in 1943, and the machine was operational by December, just in time to receive messages that prove that Hitler had been fooled by misinformation of a phantom army, commanded by General Patton, in South East England.


It is generally considered by many that the work carried out in Bletchley Park shortened the war by two to four years, and saved millions of lives.

The legacy of 'Station X' influenced every single attempt at coded messages from that moment forward.

Every computer in the world, in every form, owes their existence to the mathematic boffins at Bletchley Park.

**Due to proximity and a mix of similar interests, many Bletchley marriages took place. Most never discussed their work for decades**

## A Purposeful Disclaimer

To preserve the German's ideas of the infallibility of the Enigma machines, the allies deliberately did not act on most of the messages. If they had acted on every piece of intelligence, the Germans would have quickly determined their codes had been broken and begun working under new ones. This inaction allowed the deaths of hundreds, maybe thousands of allied troops. But it was and still is considered a necessary evil. It was paramount that the Germans be lulled into a false sense of security, thus giving away more and more information.

Some criticism has been levied at the War Office for this inaction, but like the bombs on Hiroshima and Nagasaki, it was necessary to preserve the German's view of the Enigma and Lorenz codes as infallible.

War is not a gentleman's sport.

# THE LITTLE BOATS AND OPERATION DYNAMO

With typical audacity and forward thinking, Churchill began to plan the evacuation of the BEF as early as the 20th May (just 10 days after the first German attack), calling it 'Operation Dynamo'. British Vice Admiral Bertram Ramsay was set in charge of the operation under the direct command of Churchill himself. It was the first of hundreds of military operations Winston Churchill handled personally during the entire duration of the war.

On that first day, Brigadier Gerald Whitfield was sent across the channel to Dunkirk to start evacuating unnecessary personnel. What he witnessed there shocked and horrified him. The town was in chaos, the port and beaches were filled with soldiers and officers, their mission forgotten, their arms and ammunition discarded. Despite orders to the contrary, men were boarding boats indiscriminately, their units broken up in the fog of war. In numerous cases, officers ordered to organize the boarding of troops, simply walked onto the ships themselves.

It was a complete shambles.

The French destroyer, Bourrasque, hit by mine and artillery, May 30th, 1940

On 22nd May, with this new information to hand, Churchill ordered the fighting remnants of the BEF to attack with the French First Army and hold their position. By this time the men in Dunkirk were now starving, cold, and under constant bombardment from German guns and the dive-bombing Stukas of the Luftwaffe.

The full extent of the Dunkirk situation was not told to the British public for fear of driving their morale lower, but the King George VI attended a service held in Westminster Abbey on 26th May, in which he declared it a national day of prayer. In every church, chapel and prayer house in Britain, prayers were sent to the troops, in their direst, darkest hour.

Elsewhere in France, sporadic fighting still continued, again taking German eyes and ordnance away from Dunkirk. Nearby Calais, held by the BEF, surrendered on the 26th May, the French Army, faced by seven German divisions eventually surrendered at Lille on the 31st May, their vast numbers reduced to just 35,000 available men. The Belgians surrendered on the 28th May, and tattered forces of the BEF had to rush to the north of Dunkirk to plug the gap.

The RAF were also making things 'hot' for the Germans. Although their presence was not felt on the beaches by the soldiers on the ground, they flew thousands of sorties, and made heavy kills against the bombers attacking the Dunkirk area.

Chaos on the beaches near Dunkirk. Some small boats rowed back to England

On the 26th May, after four days of fighting near Dunkirk, Churchill's Operation Dynamo eventually swung into action. From the 22nd to 26th May, just 28,000 men had been brought safely back to Britain. Even Churchill's most optimistic estimate expected no more than 45,000 to be rescued before the Germans broke through. The system had to be changed, and quickly. Thinking the worst, Churchill spoke to the House of Commons warning of "hard and heavy tidings" to come from Europe.

On the 27th, the first real day of 'Operation Dynamo', forty Royal Navy ships were involved in the rescue attempt, including eight destroyers and one cruiser. But getting large ships in and out of the Dunkirk harbor was difficult, and under constant bombing, fraught with danger. The effort was simply too slow to do any major good.

Under Churchill's orders Naval volunteers scoured British harbors for smaller boats to ferry the men to the larger vessels, and soon an Emergency broadcast asked for help from the British public. By the 31st, over 500 small boats were involved either ferrying men to the larger ships, or just dogging back and forth across the channel, bringing men directly home.

On the 30th May, Churchill eventually received news that all of the surviving BEF and half the French army were now in the Dunkirk pocket. All the eggs were in the one basket, and all they had to do was bring them home. However, Churchill's Chiefs of staff were not despondent, by this time over 150,000 men had been rescued, way beyond their original estimate, mostly from the Dunkirk harbor, but at least 70,000 from the beaches themselves.

Considering Churchill's initial estimate of 45,000 total, over 68,000 men were rescued on May 31st alone, and 64,000 the day after. But the Germans had started to close the pocket, and with the surrender of all other allied forces, were able to devote their full effort against Dunkirk. On June 2nd, the constant daytime bombing from the Luftwaffe kept evacuations to a minimum. However, under the cover of darkness that night, with the aid of the small boats, another 26,000 men were evacuated. The soldiers faced fighting and bombings the next day, but on the night of 3rd June, a further 27,000 were whisked from the harbor and beaches.

The 4th June was the last night the small boats sailed, before the Germans overwhelmed the French defenders, a further 22,000 men were saved, leaving 40,000 men of the French Army to surrender the next day.

The final figures simply beggar belief.

Almost 340,000 men were taken to safety in just nine days.

That's 1 man every 2 seconds for the entire nine days of the rescue; 1800 men every hour, day and night, 40,000 every day.

Now the brave men of the Royal Navy and Royal Air Force must be thanked. But also, many medals were won by the British public. Many civilian men and women died getting those men back to safety.

Of the 700 ships and boats deployed in the action, 226 were sunk.

But the British losses did not stop with ships and aircraft. Left behind in the rush to survive were 450 tanks, 2500 pieces of artillery, 20,000 motorcycles, and 65,000 other military vehicles. The men had survived, but without their equipment, they could hardly be called an army.

A black day indeed.

On 4th June, in a speech to the House of Commons, Churchill told the whole country that "We must be very careful not to assign to this deliverance the attributes of a victory. Wars are not won by evacuations."

With their backs firmly to the wall, Churchill and a secret coterie in the Defense Department put various measures into place, it would be the birth of many of Churchill's secret armies.

I will attempt to write them in date order, but as so many ideas were spawned concurrently, I doubt I will please everyone.

# OPERATION CYCLE & OPERATION ARIEL

### Operation Cycle & Operation Ariel

Operations Cycle and Ariel have been over-shadowed by the better-known evacuation from Dunkirk for many years (Operation Dynamo). I place the chapter not as a direct one of Churchill's Secret Armies, but as an addition to the previous chapter. And I feel this little-known phase of Britain's history needs to find its place of prominence.

On June 4th, 1940, the final boats made their way across the channel from Dunkirk, taking the remnants of the escaping British and French soldiers. But fighting carried on. On June 5th, the Germans attacked resisting French forces, and pushed towards Paris. (Little knowing the route had gaped open days earlier) The French forces resisted but the Germans, with vastly superior ground and air forces, walked into Paris on June 14th.

### Operation Cycle 10th-13th June, 1940

British forces cut off from escape at Dunkirk, terribly disorganized and ill equipped, fled westwards along the coast, making for Le Havre. The 51st Highland Division, assisted by General De Gaule's tanks fought a bloody rearguard against Rommel. Then, with the port of Le Havre suddenly cut off, the allies fled to St Valery-En-Caux where Operation Cycle was ready to embark them.

There would be no flotilla of little boats this time, under cover by the RAF, the men were transferred at the port onto destroyers, and civilian ships, commandeered for the purpose, and ferried off the beaches. From 10th-11th June, 2137 British, and 1184 French were rescued from St Valery before the rest were captured.

The men who had managed to reach Le Havre fared better.

From the 10th – 13th June, over 11,000 British troops were rescued from the French port..

And the relentless Germans pushed onwards, rolling British and French troops further westward.

## Operation Ariel 14th – 25th June 1940

Despite the lessons learned at Dunkirk, Operation Cycle had shown that large-scale troop embarkation onto large ships could be accomplished.

Operation Ariel began in earnest on June 15th, and consisted of a flotilla of Roya Navy and Merchant Marine ships which converged on the ports of Western France. The ships were supported from southern French bases by five Royal Air Force (RAF) fighter squadrons which were further assisted by squadrons from England.

The task was to enter the major sea-ports of St Nazaire, and Nantes and rescue British, Polish and Czech troops who had been directed there.

Under Luftwaffe attack, the ships loaded troops and equipment, but disorganization made figures inaccurate. On June 17th the Luftwaffe sank the Cunard liner HMT Lancastria in the Loire estuary. The troopship had just embarked thousands of troops, RAF personnel and civilians. It is estimated that at least 3500 died in the sinking.

To conform to the terms of the Armistice on June 22nd, the evacuation of Operation Ariel officially ended on June 25th.

In all, over 191,000 troops were rescued in Operation Ariel, mainly British, Polish and Czech personnel, although accurate figures of nationalities are not known.

# THE INDEPENDENT COMPANIES

### THE BACKGROUND

In the early months of 1940, although most of Europe had declared war on Germany, and Britain and France had standing armies awaiting German advances, Hitler had his attention to the west, to Poland and the oilfields of Russia. One important resource lay to Britain's north-east; Sweden's rich iron ore was transported overland to Narvik, on Norway's rugged coast. The Baltic sea was frozen for much of the winter; the ore had been transported to Narvik for many years.

Also useful to Germany's military plans were the fish oil production plants in northern Norway.

**British troops arrive in Norway, May, 1940**

### THE INDEPENDENT COMPANIES

Realizing the importance of Norwegian interests, early in 1940, Military Intelligence MI(R), lobbied the War Office for a specialist force, trained in more guerilla-like tactics than normal forces, and specializing in fighting in colder climates. On 20th April, 1940, formal approval came from Chamberlain's War Office for the establishment in the British Army of this new force, the first of its kind. Initially formed from elite men in the Territorial Army (Reserve) units, the newly named "Independent Companies" were swiftly put into training in the Scottish highlands. This rough, cold training regime was thought to get the men ready for fighting in northern climes.

Here is a list of the Territorial Army regiments the Independent Companies were taken from.

No. 1 Independent Company from 52nd (Lowland) Division

No. 2 Independent Company from 53rd (Welsh) Division

No. 3 Independent Company from 54th (East Anglian) Division

No. 4 Independent Company from 55th (West Lancashire) Division

No. 5 Independent Company from 56th (London) Division

No. 6 Independent Company from 9th (Highland) Division

No. 7 Independent Company from 15th (Scottish) Division

No. 8 Independent Company from 18th (East Anglian) Division

No. 9 Independent Company from 38th (Welsh) Division

No. 10 Independent Company from 66th (East Lancashire) Division

Initially these troops were meant to be deployed in Norway to help resist the Nazi invasion, but unfortunately Prime Minister Chamberlain was no Winston Churchill, and soon the window for an un-resisted landing had passed; Norway surrendered on June 10th, 1940, and Germans theoretically had full control of the country.

**British troops take German prisoners in Norway, 1940**

Unfortunately for any invading force, the coast of Norway is so indented with steep-sided fjords; any transport by road is both complicated and time-consuming. Throughout the war, Allied forces had access to Norway by sea, and maintained a military threat through partisans and Norwegian units training in Britain. It is considered that continual raids and actions in Norway, kept an additional 250,000 German troops ties up, which could have had a considerable effect on any of Germany's front lines.

Commandoes train in landing craft, off the coast of Scotland, 1942. Not the Thompson machine gun, favored by the Special Forces troops

## SCISSORFORCE

With the German forces still fighting Norwegian Army, on 27th April, 1940, three detachments from the newly trained Independent Companies were sent to Norway under the command of Lieutenant Colonel Colin Gubbins. The men came from 1, 3, 4, and 5 Independent Companies, and were collectively called Scissorforce. Their aim; to prevent the newly arriving German Army occupying the towns of Bodø, Mo and Mosjøen.

The Independent Companies were intended to perform scouting actions for the British troops already in Norway, and were neither trained nor equipped for a full scale action against conventional troops. But as the regular British units began to fall back, they were forced more and more into a full scale defense.

When the German forces were reinforced, and strikes from the Luftwaffe became more persistent and effective, there was nothing left for Gubbins to prove.

British Independent Companies, Norway, 1940. Job done, having a cuppa

For three consecutive nights at the end of May, under the cover of low cloud, the British forces at Bodø were disembarked by destroyers. Colonel Gubbins left on the last destroyer on the night of 31 May.

The units were disbanded on their return to Britain, many transferred into the new elite force; the Commandoes.

# THE AUXILIARY UNITS 1; OPERATIONAL PATROLS

The Auxiliary Units was the innocuous name given to the organized British resistance to German invasion. It was new, innovative, and totally secret; the first resistance units in history to be prepared before an invasion had begun...

(And, of course, because of the aborted 'Operation Sealion', Hitler's plan for invasion, it became the only pre-organized resistance unit *never* to be used).

Over 500 units were formed, utilizing over 5000 men and women in villages and towns all over Britain.

However, it did not have an auspicious start. Section D of MI6 had been given a directive to raise a resistance force, but the sight of so many strangers looking suspicious brought great consternation to British Military Intelligence. To save any more confusion, it was decided to put the organization under military command and Peter Wilkinson was set as liaison between the new commander, and the intelligence companies involved so far, MI6, Section D and Military Intelligence (Research), MI(R).

Major Colin Gubbins was put in charge of the project, fresh from his involvement with the Independent Companies. He had served in Ireland and was an expert in guerrilla warfare. He called the unconventional warfare, 'scally-wagging'.

**Members of the Warsash Patrol in Hampshire during training.**
**Photo supplied by www.staybehinds.com**

69

## THE HISTORY

The case for successful irregular fighting forces had already been proven. In the Boer War, 1899-1902, South African irregular troops were used against the British with great success. After initial losses, the Boer commanders adopted guerrilla tactics, conducting raids against the British infrastructure, mainly in resource and supply targets, all aimed at disrupting the operational capacity of the British Army. Later in the war, the British used 'turned' Boers to form their own irregular units.

In the Middle East, T.E. Lawrence ('Lawrence of Arabia') had a great influence on British military strategists. In 1916-1918, his irregular supplement to General Allenby's troops against the Turks culminated in an Allied victory in Damascus. Lawrence had proven that passionate properly led, lightly armed troops, were more than a match for an invader unfamiliar with the battlefield.

In Ireland, from the uprising of 1916 to the treaty with the British in 1921, Michael Collins ran a spy ring far superior to the British system. Their 'cell'-like system had the British counterparts on their heels for most of the 'war'.

Officers influenced by these three campaigns were close to Churchill's ear. Their experiences would influence Britain's leader in many of the 'Secret Armies' Churchill would create in the dark months of 1940.

## THE ORIGINATOR

At the outbreak of the war, Peter Fleming, brother of Ian Fleming, creator of James Bond, worked in MI (R), Military Intelligence (Research). Peter had trekked the Brazilian jungles and taken the 3,500 mile trek from Peking to Kashmir. He was an expert on irregular units, and an advisor to the war Office.

Churchill was impressed by Fleming's idea of a small force left behind after the German Invasion who would work on a 'cell' basis, with no overriding command structure.

Local men who knew the land intimately would be perfect for such a force, going to ground on the actual invasion, and rising with the proper equipment to cause chaos behind enemy lines. Peter Fleming was given permission to start such a unit.

Peter Fleming; Ian's elder brother, and originator of the Auxiliary Units

Called 'XII Corps Observation Unit', Fleming set up the very first British 'operational resistance unit' in a lonely farmhouse called 'The Garth', near the hamlet of Bilting, in South-eastern Kent; right in the center of the likely Nazi target area. Using as much information as he could draw to hand, Fleming trained his troops in close quarter combat, demolition, and counter espionage.

In June 1940, in the wake of Dunkirk, Churchill decided to throw full resources behind the forming of a network of Auxiliary Units. The structure was to be under the command of Major Colin Gubbins, who would eventually be linked with several of Churchill's Secret Armies. When Peter Wilkinson was given the job to organize the structure of the Auxiliary Units, he held up Peter Fleming's unit as a model, and soon duplicated it up and down the coast.

An old Intelligence operator, Andrew Croft, was chosen for the next hub, and was responsible for Essex and Suffolk. Moving north, again old friends were used, and John Gwynne, a friend of Peter Fleming's, was chosen to head East Anglia. The organization almost spread quicker than Wilkinson could comprehend, and within two months, over 500 separate independent cells had been structured, from South Wales to Brechin in Scotland.

With no legal backing, and funded secretly by the War cabinet, nothing of its like had ever been tried before.

The inside of an Operational Base (OB)

## HOW IT ALL WORKED

On a local level, the organization began with the choice of team leader. It had to be a local person of relative standing; a farmer, a landowner, a parish priest or vicar. This 'sergeant' had to be someone who had their own transport, and who would be inconspicuous having petrol to drive around in a time of hardship and rationing. Five or six locals would be recruited, directed to the sergeant, and the cell was complete. Members were generally men (some teenagers or boy scouts as young as 15) of 'reserve' occupations, farmers, coal workers, gamekeepers; men who by their profession were exempt from normal service in the Army, and would not call attention to themselves by not being 'called up'.

Using the now well-known 'cell' format, no one in the network knew the identity of any member of any other group. They were warned NOT to contact any British Army unit, they were to remain hidden and operate in a 5-10 mile circle round their village.

Each unit was then directed to dig their own underground operating base to an accurate blueprint. This Operating Base, (OB), would be in woods, in dense thickets, or even in gardens and under houses. Blindfolded local builders and Army engineers then delivered the arched corrugated roof, and built the brick-built grenade-proof shaft. The Units would then back-fill the hole, disguising the shaft entrance and roof.

Operational Base (OB), showing air vent, hatch, living quarters and escape

Over 500 of these OB's were built in a matter of months in 1940.

The completed OB had a shaft with ladder, leading to a living area with six to eight bunk beds. In the case of imminent invasion, a code word "Oliver" would be broadcast on the BBC radio. This would be the code to send the auxiliary units to ground, to their OB's. If the code word "Cromwell" followed, it would mean the invasion had been a success; the war had arrived.

Auxiliaries would wait in hiding until the fighting passed overhead, and then arise to cause as much trouble and destruction of enemy personnel and equipment as they could before being caught or killed. Their life expectancy after invasion was said to be between two and three weeks. These men were the last line of defense in an occupied Britain. Their mission? To kill, sabotage and cause mayhem behind enemy lines, to destroy ammunition dumps, petrol dumps, aircraft, bridges, locomotives, anything to disrupt the Nazi war machine.

The recruits would attend basic training at various regional training centers all over Britain, but the most famous is in Highworth. Recruits would report to the silver-haired postmistress, Mabel Stranks, Highworth, near Surrey, the Auxiliary Unit's secret 'gateway'. Over 3500 reported to Mabel in 1940 alone. Training given at Coleshill House, just three miles away, included close quarter killing, demolition, explosives, sniper instruction; almost every aspect of counter-espionage.

**Specifications of the Sykes-Fairbairn silent killing knife**

Showing their importance, the Auxiliary troops were equipped better than any other army unit of the time. They were issued with Fairbairn knives, a 0.22 sniper rifle, and new Thomson machine guns, at a time when the Home Guard drilled with broom handles. With the shortage of rifles after Dunkirk, it was decided to outfit the Auxiliary Units with the American Springfield M1903 (30.03). The rifles could not fire the standard Lee Endfield 3.03 round anyway, and the war Office had enough Springfield rifles and ammunition to go round.

Auxiliary Units were given thousands of tons of plastic Explosive, specially designed for them, detonators, and many new 'gadgets' dreamed up by the technical departments of the intelligence services. It was not uncommon for a single unit to have two or three hundred pounds of explosive, delayed action fuses, grenades, smoke bombs, and many different types of detonator.

Auxiliaries spent their days working as normal, and their nights doing dummy attack runs into army bases and airfields.

It is widely accepted that these troops were the best equipped and trained British soldiers of the day; many joined elite battalions later in the war.

But their role upon invasion would not be a pretty one. On the first few days after the German soldiers passed overhead, the Auxiliary Units first task would be to assassinate the local police chiefs, keeping vital information out of German hands. Next in line were the men who had recruited them, men who knew their true identities. This was a planned war of a dirty nature, not pretty times at all.

Anthony Quayle, English Actor, was a British Army officer, and regional commander of the Auxiliary Units in Northumberland; if Britain had been invaded, he would have been one of the first to be shot.

Every guerilla or terrorist organization can trace some of their organization's training or operations back to the training of the SOE and the Auxiliary Units.

By mid-November, 1941, the threat of imminent invasion had lessened, the Battle of Britain had been won by the RAF, and the role of the Auxiliary Units was greatly diminished. Major Colin Gubbins was taken from direct control, and with Wilkinson in tow, left for a head role in the newly formed SOE.

### THE AUXILIARY UNITS 2; SPECIAL DUTIES SECTION

Run separately from the Auxiliary Units' standard 'resistance' Operational Patrols was the Special Duty Branch. This organization, containing around 4000 people, was originally recruited by the intelligence services, (mostly SIS and SOE) and were members of the local people carefully vetted and selected for either their access to the population or position in the community. This organization acted as the eyes and ears of the intelligence services and would report back to military intelligence any information they heard considered to be 'careless talk'. Members of the SDS had been trained to identify military vehicles, high-ranking officers and military units, and were to gather intelligence and leave reports in dead letter drops. The reports would be collected by runners and taken to one of over 200 secret radio transmitters operated by trained civilian signals staff located all over Britain. The wireless network was hoped to be still working after invasion and would double as a subversive network.

# THE BRITISH SPECIAL OPERATIONS EXECUTIVE (SOE)

In the spring of 1940, Britain relied on three independent agencies for counter espionage work, each with their own personalities, their own champions, and their own budgets. Some communication between these agencies took place as the men knew each other well, but some work was duplicated; it made absolute sense to bring the three agencies together;

One leadership.

One building.

One budget.

One place to trace leaks to.

The Secret Intelligence Service (SIS) was formed in 1909, an idea of both the War Department and the Admiralty. During the First World War the SIS spied on enemy shipping, and eventually the foreign arm became known as the Directorate of Military Intelligence, Section 6 (or MI6 for short). With the aim of sabotage and subversion, plans were drawn to send agents behind enemy lines, but they lacked a coherent plan. In March 1938 they set up department D (D for dirty tricks) to investigate both propaganda and sabotage against Germany.

Set up in March 1938, a propaganda organization known as Department EH (after Electra House, its headquarters) existed within the Foreign Office. It was also known as CS, and studied anti-Nazi propaganda and leafletting.

The third spy department was a dual based agency inside the War Office. In the autumn of 1938, the War Office expanded an existing research department known as GS (R) to conduct research into guerrilla and irregular warfare. GS (R) was renamed MI (R) in early 1939.

When all three organisations were given premises in 64 Baker Street, London, there would be a short period of interdepartmental bickering before they all settled down to work in unison. (The members called their membership the "Baker Street Irregulars")

Initially, the SOE divided itself into two sections; SO1, responsible for propaganda, and SO2, responsible for subversion and sabotage. As the organization grew, SO1 became the Political Welfare Executive (PWE) in Aug 1941.

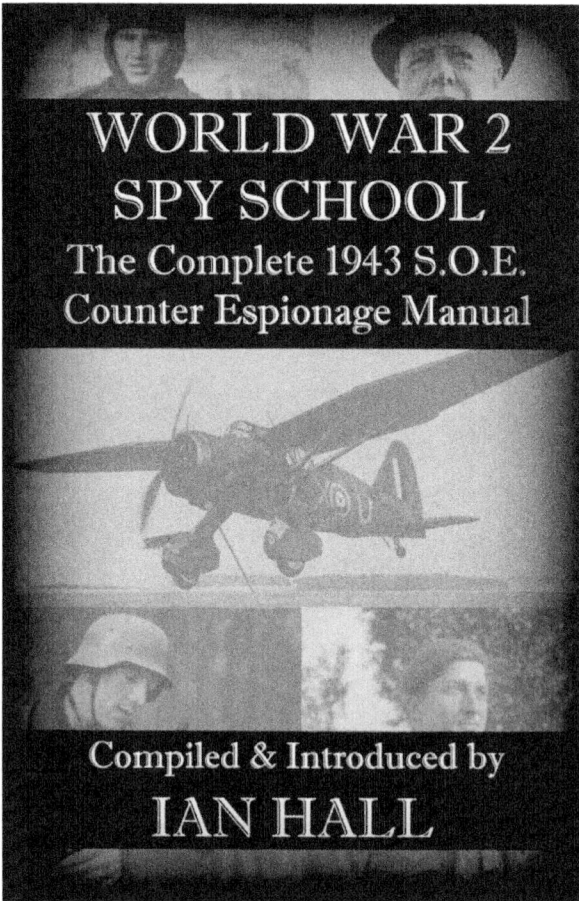

WORLD WAR 2
SPY SCHOOL
The Complete 1943 S.O.E.
Counter Espionage Manual

Compiled & Introduced by
IAN HALL

My own book; a full transcript of the 1943 SOE training manual

### THE SOE MANUAL

The SOE decided that the new organization should have a standard working training manual for all recruits and instructors to follow. Plans were put in place for bases in North America and Asia, but first they had to find premises in the UK.

The SOE syllabus was first written in 1940 and adapted and expanded as the war continued. Over a thousand agents passed the classes and went on to work behind enemy lines in every theatre of the war.

The actual 'nuts and bolts' of the manual is ascribed to Paul Dehn who already operated within SOE. Dehn was a film critic before the war and later worked with fellow SOE member Ian Fleming (the creator of James Bond), and wrote the screenplays for *Goldfinger*, and *Murder on the Orient Express*.

The manual was a masterful work.

In over 400 pages, its lessons would take a common man from the streets and teach him to be a top secret agent, capable of operating behind enemy lines in the most dangerous of situations. It would deal with such topics as espionage, counter intelligence, disguises, forming cells, and codes and cyphers. It gave an overview of the German military, gestapo, and local police units. It was updated regularly as new information became available on current war situations. It would be the spy and espionage blueprint of the war, and was classified for many years.

## THE RECRUITS

From inception, the recruits chosen were young men and women. Their age varied, but on the whole, priority was given to agents between 19 and 26. The emphasis on youth was on purpose; young people had less a far lesser amount of fear; their feeling of invulnerability gave them an advantage over older subjects. On the whole, once an agent had reached 30 years of age, they were 'retired' to the ranks of training staff. Once a person reached 30, it seemed they had lost their 'edge'.

## SOE STATIONS

At the height of the war, the SOE had many establishments in Britain, divided into three categories.

### Experimental Bases

Located mostly in Hertfordshire for its close proximity to London, establishments working with experimental devices, new developments, storage and production were allocated Roman numeral names.

Station VI - Bride Hall near Ayot St Lawrence, Hertfordshire.

Weapons acquisition section, both for foreign and domestic weapons.

Station VIIa - Bontex Knitting Mills, Beresford Avenue, Wembley.

Wireless Production Section, building and developing new covert radio equipment.

Station VIIb - Yeast-Vite factory, Whippendell Road, Watford.

Wireless Packing Section, packing into final suitcases, and dispatch.

Station VIIc - Allensor's joinery factory, King George's Avenue, Watford.

Wireless Research Section.

Section VIId - Kay's garage, Bristol Street, Birmingham.

Wireless Production Section.

Station IX - Frythe estate near Welwyn Garden City.

Began as a wireless research unit (Special Signals), then moved to weapons development & production, then a research and development station.

Station IXa - P O Box 1, Ashford, Middlesex.

Submersible Section, located at Staines reservoir.

Station IXc - Fishguard Bay Hotel, Goodwick, Pembrokeshire.

Submersibles Station, located in Fishguard Bay.

Station XI - Old Gorhambury House near St Albans, Hertfordshire.

Accommodation.

Station XII - Aston House near Stevenage, Hertfordshire.

Production, packaging and dispatch.

Station XIV - Briggens, near Roydon, Essex.

Forgery Section.

Station XV - The Thatched Barn, Borehamwood, Hertfordshire.

Camouflage Section. The final equipping of agents prior to going to France

Station XVa - 56 Queen's Gate, Kensington, London SW7 - Camouflage Section - prototypes.

Station XVb - The Demonstration Room, Natural History Museum in London.

Camouflage Section , training center for agents.

Station XVc - 2-3 Trevor Square, Knightsbridge, South Kensington.

Camouflage Section, dealing with photographic and make-up section.

Station XVII - Brickendonbury, Brickendon, Hertford.

Explosive Experimenting and Testing Station.

STS 26. Demonstration for King Haakon, Glenmore Lodge, Aviemore, Scotland

## Training Schools

Over 50 schools all around Britain, some general, many specialized, given Arabic STS codes.

STS 1 - Brock Hall, Flore, Northamptonshire

STS 2 - Bellasis, Box Hill Road, Dorking, Surrey. Used for the training of ex-German PoWs, training and holding center for Czech section.

STS 3 - Stodham Park, Liss, Hampshire. Specialized in mines and the use/training of enemy weapons.

STS 5 - Wanborough Manor, Puttenham, Guildford, Surrey. Initial training establishment for SOE operatives ('F', French, Section).

STS 6 - West Court, Finchampstead, Wokingham, Berkshire.

STS 7 (formerly STS 4) - Winterfold, Cranleigh, Surrey. Students Assessment Board.

STS 14 - Briggins, Roydon, Essex.

STS 17 - Brickendonbury Manor. School of sabotage.

STS 19 - Gardener's End, Ardeley, Stevenage, Hertfordshire.

STS 20a & 20b - Pollards Park House, Chalfont St Giles. Polish section.

STS 21 - Arisaig House, Arisaig, Inverness-shire. Commando-style training.

STS 22a - Glasnacardoch Lodge, Mallaig, Inverness-shire. Weapons servicing store.

STS 23 - Meoble Lodge, beside Loch Morar, Inverness-shire.

STS 23b - Swordland, Tarbet Bay, beside Loch Morar, Inverness-shire.

STS 24a - Inverie House, Knoydart, near Mallaig, Inverness-shire.

STS 24b - Glaschoille, Knoydart, Mallaig, Inverness-shire.

STS 25a - Garramor, South Morar, Inverness-shire.

STS 25b - Camusdarach, South Morar, Inverness-shire.

STS 25c - Traigh House, South Morar, Inverness-shire.

STS 26 - Drumintoul Lodge, Aviemore, Inverness-shire and Glenmore Lodge, Inverness-shire. Norwegian Holding School . HQ for Linge Company.

SOE STS 31, at Beaulieu House, Hampshire

STS 31 to STS 27b - Beaulieu, Hampshire. Finishing schools.

STS 31 - The Rings, Beaulieu, Hampshire. Security training school.

STS 36 - Boarmans, Beaulieu, Hampshire.

STS 40 - Howbury Hall, Waterend, Bedford. Training in use of aircraft S-Phone.

STS 41 - Gumley Hall, Market Harborough.

STS 42 - Roughwood Park, Chalfont St Giles, Bucks.

STS 43 - Audley End House, Essex - Polish section.

STS 44 - Water Eaton Manor, Oxford.

STS 45 - Hatherop Castle, Fairford, Gloucestershire. Danish holding school and HQ.

STS 46 - Chichely Hall, Buckinghamshire. Czechoslovak Section.

STS 49 -Forthampton House, Tewkesbury, Gloucestershire.

STS 50 - Gorse Hill, Witley, Surrey.

STS 51 - Dunham House, Altrincham, Cheshire. Parachute training (near RAF Ringway)

STS 51b - Fulshaw Hall, Wilmslow, Cheshire. Parachute training (near RAF Ringway)

STS 52 - Thame Park, Oxfordshire - security training for wireless operators

STS 53a - Grendon Hall, Aylesbury, Buckinghamshire. Signals center.

STS 53b - Poundon House, Buckinghamshire. Radio listening and transmission station.

STS 53c - Poundon, Buckinghamshire. Training American forces in SOE communications techniques.

STS 54a - Fawley Court, Henley on Thames. Signals Section (Wireless Operators).

STS 54b - Belhaven School, Dunbar. Signals Section (Wireless Operators).

STS 61 - Audley End, Saffron Walden. Packing parachute containers.

STS 61 - Gaynes' Hall, St Neots.

STS 62 - Anderson Manor, Anderson, Dorset.

STS 63 Erlestoke Park, Stately home used for 'Senior Officers' School'

## SPECIALIST TRAINING SCHOOLS (STS)

Under one roof, and with one budget, the new SOE soon saw the need for a structured series of Specialist Training Schools (STS) for the training of behind-the-lines operatives.

The training schools were set up on three distinct levels;

### Preliminary Schools

In the winter of 1940, the SOE acquired six large estate houses in the Home Counties, to house the first part of the training program. These homes were large, luxurious, but not far from the public eye.

In the ten weeks at the Preliminary Schools the students' character was assessed, both physically and mentally. The weak links were weeded out here, and did not advance in their training. Care was taken to evaluate their potential for dangerous clandestine work without actually revealing to the candidates much about their ultimate purpose. Although they were under training, details of the SOE and its work were never mentioned.

From the first day the schools covered general physical training, weapons handling, unarmed combat, elementary demolitions, map reading, fieldcraft and basic signaling. Much of this was the sort of training that any army recruit might expect to receive.

### Paramilitary Schools

The Paramilitary Schools were a notch harder, lasting about five weeks. Numbered STS 21 to STS 25, they were based in shooting lodges in the Arisaig and Morar areas of Inverness-shire. The surrounding countryside, which includes Loch Morar and Loch Nevis, is rugged and remote, ideal for the harder commando-style training that was provided. Hard physical training, silent killing, weapons handling, demolition, map reading and compass were taught, along with advanced fieldcraft, elementary Morse code, and raid tactics.

STS 23, based at Swordland, Tarbet Bay, concentrated on teaching how to use special devices when attacking ships.

STS 22, at Glasnacardoch Lodge, Mallaig, was a foreign-weapons school. Stolen weapons from Germany, France, Russia and other eastern countries were used exclusively. In one exercise weapons were stripped, then strewn on the floor in darkened rooms. Blindfolded agents had to identify their own weapon's parts, assemble the weapon, and exit the room ready to fire.

Parachute training was one of the last disciplines to learn, at an airfield (STS-51, Ringway) near Manchester. Although candidates from SOE were trained with other units, they were not allowed to converse, and ate their meals separately.

### Finishing Schools

Only when the candidates qualified to Finishing School were they told the name of their new employer, the SOE. The training now was extensive and very concentrated. The candidates ate talked and slept Morse Code. They trained in advanced explosives work, and learned how to survive behind enemy lines. When the candidates had completed the course, they were sent to a flat in London for their final briefing and assignments.

By the end of the war, there were over 50 SOE schools in the UK, employing between 1200-1400 teaching staff. Nearly 7000 students 'graduated', although only around 500 were actually British.

STS 103,Camp X, Toronto, Canada, opened the day before Pearl Harbor

## CAMPS OUTSIDE BRITAIN

From the outset, it became obvious that the camps inside the UK had limited geographical use. The Germans held mainland Europe, and their conquest of Britain seemed next. There was also no real advantage to having foreign agents-in-training sent to British camps, just to have half their unsuccessful candidates returned to their country of origin. Generally it made sense to have camps elsewhere to separate the wheat from the chaff. Once candidates had passed the initial classes, they were usually sent to Britain for further training.

**Camp STS-101** was set up in Singapore in July 1941. The office was short-lived due to the rapid surrender to the invading Japanese, but some SOE agents 'stayed behind', many fighting successfully in the jungle until the end of the war.

**Camp STS 102** was stationed at Ramat David, near Haifa, Palestine, and moved to Italy when a safe foothold had been established. STS-102 was in charge of the agents being deployed into the Mediterranean, Greece, Cyprus and the Balkans.

**Camp Sts-103 (Camp X) In Canada** was built just ten miles east of Toronto, on the shores of Lake Ontario. By the autumn of 1941, it was obvious that a good number of early candidates had come from the United States and Canada. These students already had a second language due to their French Canadian ancestry or their recent immigrant status in the USA. To save bringing every applicant over, only to have half of them fail the first training period, it was decided to set up a third foreign STS camp; Camp STS 103.

On 6th December, 1941, just one day before the Japanese Navy descended on Pearl Harbor, Hawaii, Camp STS103 opened its gates for the first intake of 'agents in training'.

William 'Wild Bill' Donovan; Roosevelt's number one man, the head of the OSS

### The SOE and OSS

The United States of America was still a neutral power in the global struggle that would be called World War 2, and would remain so for one more day.

Just six months before, in July 1941, Colonel William J. Donovan had been appointed "Coordinator of Information" (COI) at the newly formed Washington department. His blueprint for an American version of the British Secret Intelligence Service (MI6) had been approved and the fledgling department would send its first agents to Canada to be trained.

The system was hardly new. The British already had such camps in England and Scotland, but they lacked the depth of first generation immigrant that both Canada and America could readily provide. Men and women joined, ready to face hardship and life-threatening danger behind enemy lines; it was the beginning of the spy game as we know it today.

Since the FBI held a domestic jurisdiction, it was felt necessary for the USA to engage the idea of counter espionage coordination abroad, so six months later, a new department was formed, encapsulating the nucleus of the still small COI group. The new Office of Strategic Services (OSS), would take on all aspects of espionage, propaganda, subversion and post war planning. By the end of the war, it would employ over 24,000 men and women. After the war, the OSS would be the nucleus of the CIA.

All modelled on the British SOE.

**Camp Cactus on Catalina Island, off the coast of California**

## The Rise Of Camps In The USA

Using Camp X as a model, the American OSS soon opened seven camps in Maryland and Virginia, designated Training Area's A,B,C,D,E,F, and the Farm. Thousands of trainees would go through their gates, trained under the original SOE manual.

The largest of these camps were Prince William Forest, near Quantico, Virginia, and Catoctin Mountain Park, in Maryland.

Catoctin (B-2) was opened on April 1st, 1942. Its capacity in October 1943 was 20 officers and 130 enlisted men.

The SOE kidnapped German General Heinrich Kreipe in Crete, 1944

## THE SOE; THE ORGANIZATION THAT WON THE WAR

The effect the SOE had on World War 2 and any counter espionage from that date cannot be properly defined. Before its inception, no organization had the resources, scope, experience and mastery of espionage and counter espionage of the SOE. It was the founder, innovator and model for every spy/intelligence organization since 1940. The SOE training manual became the founding document for all global espionage and counter espionage, and every terrorist group on the planet.

Colin Gubbins was probably the most under-celebrated officer of the war, and the world owes a great debt to the diminutive man.

In a time of instability and threat, the SOE took the war to the axis powers. They assisted in military raids in personnel, training and intelligence. They broke a German spy network to the stage that every single German spy in Britain was a double agent, sending bogus information back to the Nazi High Command. They sent thousands of recruits behind enemy lines with such effect that when Churchill told them to "set Europe ablaze", they actually did.

'Silent Killing'; the Sykes-Fairbairn knife. Fairbairn aged 57, trained recruits

Based on the idea that every single German soldier who was occupied away from the front lines was one less man for the regular army to face, they tied Hitler's forces in knots, keeping literally millions of men from regular active duty.

It is considered that in the Balkans alone, the partisan resistance faced as many German troops as the whole Allied Army in the Italian Campaign. The SOE were a thorn in Hitler's side that he could not eradicate.

## The SOE Cell

SOE agents were usually sent behind enemy lines in pairs, each trained to do the other's job if captured or killed. Unless they were involved in a specific mission, their job was to integrate themselves into the local area, and gather men and women passionate on killing the enemy.

The leader would recruit partisans to his 'cell', being careful to fully vet the person concerned; Nazi double agents and sympathizers were common. Few people in the cell knew everyone, until the day of the operation. Communication within the cell was done by dead drops, using children to deliver messages, or by more complex means.

The most important man in the group was the radio operator. In case of capture, wherever possible, he *never* carried the radio. In the early years of the war communication was sporadic, disorganized, but as the years progressed and the number of agents behind the lines grew, each operator then had a specific time to communicate and receive messages.

Information was broadcast by the BBC radio services, containing hours of short chunky sentences, mostly meaning nothing to anyone. Then, alerted by a code word, the listening operator received a cryptic message. The simple phrase "Winter tulips are early this year, cover them", might mean the operation had been moved forward, kill the gestapo chief.

German radio-detector vans worked tirelessly to find transmitting sets. Located inside a small suitcase, the radio could be set up or dismantled in minutes. Many an operator escaped capture by a margin of seconds.

## Resistance Building

One of the main functions of SOE agents behind enemy lines was to build a successful partisan resistance. Agents were trained to coerce reluctant locals into fighting their occupying forces, and trained the men and women on site. They supplied information, guns and ammunition, explosives and detonators, disguises, false papers, maps, targets, everything a clandestine operation needed to cause misery and mayhem to a German occupying force already stretched to breaking point.

SOE Operative, Christine Granville (Krystyna Skarbek) in France 1944

Typical of the SOE attention-to-detail was reproducing 'authentic' French clothing which was copied from existing designs, newspaper photographs, catalogues etc. The work had to be perfect down to the last stitch and button. Stations in Hertfordshire hand sewed maps into silk underwear. Papers and documents were forged with unbelievable accuracy, letters, receipts from local stores, money and coinage.

Booby traps were manufactured and distributed; false dead rats with a small explosive inside, bicycle pumps which exploded when used, hand grenades encapsulated into tins labelled as fruit. Plaster of Paris was molded and painted to resemble a log; inside was a Sten gun.

In the early hours of D-day, 6th June, 1944, nearly 1000 separate SOE operations took place behind enemy lines; it was a wonder of organization. Communications were cut in hundreds of locations, bridges bombed, railway lines destroyed, key emplacements attacked, and vital officers shot or captured. Without the mass of SOE operations, and Operation Jedburgh (which also involved the SOE), working behind the lines, creating mayhem and cutting communications, countless more allied men would have died on that day and the days afterwards.

**Propaganda**

The recruits were trained in the art of propaganda, not only to win hearts and minds and gain allies while behind enemy lines, but also to influence whole populations. Operatives used information and misinformation successfully to influence local people to join partisan groups and fight for their country's liberation. They also gathered information from the occupying forces and use it to their advantage, distributing subversive documents which cut at the morale of the troops, and threw doubt into their belief system, training and leadership.

An SOE Operative places explosives on a railway line

### Espionage

Bringing explosives and detonators in the tens of thousands, the SOE agents performed demolitions, or trained others to do so. Initially they destroyed railway lines, but found them soon repaired and normal railway travel rapidly re-established. They quickly changed tactics, blowing up bridges instead. This meant the Germans had to guard every single major bridge in Europe, and some of the smaller ones, twenty-four hours per day. It is estimated that this task alone, just guarding bridges, kept half a million Axis troops away from the front lines.

### Assassination

Many thousands of murders, killings and personal attacks were carried out by SOE agents and their cells during the war. It was a brutal time, and no quarter was given. If agents were caught, they were usually interrogated, shot or both. The lucky ones got thrown in prison or concentration camps. Hundreds of agents died, and many thousands of partisans.

The most famous assassination was the SOE attack on SS-Obergruppenführer und General der Polizei, Reinhard Heydrich, the head of the German Gestapo.

Heydrich was attacked in Prague on 27 May 1942 by a SOE/British-trained team of Czech soldiers in Operation Anthropoid. Jozef Gabčík and Jan Kubiš were sent to Czechoslovakia in December, 1941, and although they could not perform the pre-planned operation, they later travelled to Prague and improvised. Catching Heydrich on a familiar route in his car, they intended to open fire with Sten machine guns. When his gun jammed, Kubiš threw a modified anti-tank grenade at the car and shrapnel injured Heydrich. The gestapo leader would later die of his wounds.

The SOE had struck into the core of Nazi Germany, taking out Adolf Hitler's number 2.

### SOE'S DIVISIONS/SECTIONS

Any private company or organization that attempts to do everything, will either fail, or subdivide to allow different departments to tackle different facets of the subject or problem.

The SOE was no different. From the moment of its inception, the internal structure of the SOE fractured into three parts, then subdivided again, new departments being created to deal personally and directly with the many facets of the mass operation it was created to face. It spawned so many other organizations, its true scope may never be fully realized.

**Anthony Quayle, Ian Fleming, and Christopher Lee, all worked for the SOE**

Celebrities who are said to have either worked with or for the SOE;

**Anthony Quayle**; after being an Auxiliary Unit regional commander in Northumbria, Quayle moved to the SOE, where he became a liaison with partisans in Albania.

**Ian Fleming**, author of James Bond and Chitty Chitty Bang Bang, worked for many intelligence networks. It is thought that he coordinated with the SOE on numerous occasions, and attended Camp STS 103 in Canada.

**Roald Dahl** is rumored to have trained at Camp X (STS 103), but it is known that he worked for British Intelligence in New York, writing and giving speeches on behalf of BSC, encouraging the USA to join the war.

**Christopher Lee** has been silent about his wartime exploits, but he is known to have said he worked for the SOE and LRDG.

**Paul Dehn**, film critic before the war, and friend of Ina Fleming, was screenwriter of *Goldfinger*, *Murder on the Orient Express*, and the *Planet of the Apes* sequels. He is known to have written most, if not all of the SOE Training Manual. He also visited Camp X (STS 103) in Canada.

**Hardy Aimes**, dressmaker to Queen Elizabeth II and designer of her wedding dress, joined SOE in 1940, rising to Section Head of the Belgian Section.

# THE LONG RANGE DESERT GROUP

**David Stirling, the originator of the LRDG and the SAS**

The idea of this special operations group was the brainchild of David Stirling.

Originally called the Long Range Patrol (LRP), the Long Range Desert Group (LRDG) was founded in Egypt in June 1940 by Major Ralph Bagnold, under General Archibald Wavell.

**Major Ralph Bagnold** was well used to life in the British army. His father had participated in the rescue of General Gordon in Khartoum. His sister was the novelist and playwright Enid Bagnold, who wrote the 1935 novel National Velvet.

Bagnold was an explorer and pioneer of desert travel by motor vehicle, and is credited with inventing the sun compass. He also developed a fast way to drive over the Libyan "sand seas", much used by the LRP. At the outbreak of the war, Bagnold was in Cairo, and approached General Wavell to use his experience to form a quick strike scouting team to perform missions behind Italian lines. With permission in his pocket, he chose his command officers carefully.

**Captain William Boyd Kennedy Shaw** (British) explored the Libyan Desert as botanist, archaeologist and navigator in the 1920s and 1930s. He and Bagnold had worked together for years, and when the war broke out, Bagnold travelled to Palestine to recruit Kennedy Shaw, who was working for the government. Kennedy Shaw first enlisted for the Intelligence Corps, but as soon as the LRP was commissioned, he switched. During the war he served in GSO 2 (Intelligence) and in 1944 joined the SAS.

Two LRDG patrols meet. The Italians called them The Ghost Patrol

**Captain Patrick Clayton** (British) had been a surveyor in Egypt in the 1920's and 1930's, and was drafted back to the country by Bagnold for his local knowledge. Initially commissioned into the Intelligence Corps, he was co-opted by Bagnold into the LRP. He was the basis for the character of Peter Madox in *The English Patient*, a 1992 novel by Michael Ondaatje.

Initially the vast majority of LRP recruits were from New Zealand, but they were soon bolstered by Rhodesian and British volunteers. When the units grew, they were divided into sub-units and the name was changed to the now well-known Long Range Desert Group (LRDG).

Long Range Desert group, showing their converted Chevrolet trucks

The LRDG was never intended as a strike force, and were formed to carry out deep penetrating drives, covert reconnaissance patrols and intelligence missions behind Italian lines. Because of the officers' experience, the LRDG were experts in desert navigation and were assigned to guide other units, including the Special Air Service and secret agents across the desert.

The LRDG initially used what vehicles they could find, but were soon supplied with brand new Chevrolet trucks, which they fitted with bristling machine guns, and adapted the engines for desert driving. Willy's Jeeps for the Commanders completed the line-up.

They were so elusive to the Italian soldiers, they called the LRDG *The Ghost Patrol*.

Between December 1940 and April 1943, the vehicles of the LRDG operated constantly behind the Axis lines, observing enemy movements, convoys, and transmitting the intelligence to British Army Headquarters.

When the German Afrika Corps surrendered in Tunisia in May 1943, the LRDG moved their operations to the eastern Mediterranean, carrying out missions in the Greek islands, Italy and the Balkans.

After the end of the war in Europe, the LRDG was disbanded in August 1945.

**A LRDG patrol, driving their American Willys Jeeps**

The LRDG were the basis of the television series *The Rat Patrol*, in the 1960's

# THE BRITISH SECURITY COORDINATION (BSC)

**William Donovan, pinning the Medal of Merit on William Stephenson, (BSC)**

William Samuel Stephenson was born in Manitoba, Canada, in 1897. He served in the Canadian Army and Air Force in the First World War, and was a Flying Ace. Many think of Stephenson as the blueprint for Ian Fleming's character, James Bond.

On 20th June, 1940, Winston Churchill sent Stephenson to the USA to set up the British Security Coordination (BSC). BSC, located at Room 3603, Rockefeller Center, New York City, would be directly responsible to MI6 and would act as the 'overseer' of the American operations of MI5 (Military Intelligence, Home based), MI6 (Military Intelligence, Foreign based), SOE (Special Operations Executive) and PWE (Political Warfare Executive).

Its remit;

Investigate all enemy activities in the western hemisphere.

Provide security for British properties against enemy attack, sabotage, infiltration, etc.

BSC occupied a whole floor of the Rockefeller Building, New York. Posing as British Passport Control, the BSC waged a war within America

Encourage American popular opinion to send aid and supplies to a beleaguered Britain, and to encourage USA to join the war against the Nazis.

Stephenson's official title was that of British Passport Control Officer, although any actual passport duties were performed by office clerks. His unofficial mission, given by Churchill himself, was to create and operate a new secret British intelligence network throughout the whole of the western hemisphere, North America, South America and the Caribbean. Working for the British Government and the allies, he was America's spy-master, responsible for the complete spy network in the Americas.

With an introduction by Churchill, Stephenson worked with, and became an advisor of the American president, Theodore Roosevelt.

**Newspapers**

The BSC influenced many of the top American newspapers, having agents within the organizations. It is known that they had heavy influence in the Herald Tribune, the New York Post, and The Baltimore Sun, and it is suspected that they had fingers working in many more.

Radio

Regular radio broadcasts were given the BSC slant, encouraging a new perspective on America's isolationism. Radio stations throughout the country were influenced.

The British Security Coordination had many notable employees.

### David Ogilvy

Now seen as the father of modern advertising, Englishman Ogilvy was also the man who first applied the Gallup polling technique to the BSC fields of military intelligence.

### Eric Maschwitz

Maschwitz was an entertainer, broadcaster, and wrote the words of A Nightingale sang in Berkley Square.

Fleming travelled to America in 1941, meeting with William 'Wild Bill' Donovan

### Ian Fleming

Yet again Fleming's name turns up. He was well known by Bill Donovan and wrote papers for the OSS giant.

### C. S. Forrester

C. S. Forrester, the author of *Hornblower* novel series and *The African Queen* (adapted for a movie starring Humphrey Bogart and Katherine Hepburn) worked for Stephenson at the Rockefeller building.

C. S. Forrester, already a popular novelist, worked at the BSC with Roald dahl

Forrester was introduced to Roald Dahl, a pilot ace from the air war over Greece. Forrester was told to ask Dahl for some RAF anecdotes to write into a story, Dahl's action account was released unedited, and was Dahl's first ever written work.

Roald Dahl (left with RAF uniform), with Ernest Hemmingway, in 1944

# THE COMMANDOES

When he first came to power as Prime Minister, Winston Churchill already had the nucleus in place for an elite force.

**Version 1: The Independent Companies**

The British Commandoes can trace their birth to these units. Formed in the April of 1940, and already training in the Scottish Highlands, ready for use against the Germans in Norway. Chamberlain, to Churchill's annoyance, had failed to deploy them before the Nazis invaded Norway. Although the optimal time had passed, Churchill rubber-stamped their joining the fight, already in progress, but their use was limited.

Independent Companies with German prisoners, Norway, 1940

When the independent Companies came back from deployment in Norway, they disbanded, most of them going back to their old units.

Churchill realized with the ignominy of defeat at Dunkirk, both the Army and the British people needed a shot in the arm, a raising of morale. He needed to strike back quickly. He called for the Independent Companies to be deployed in Norway and to hit the Germans along the French coast.

But Churchill wanted more.

### Version 2; Special Duty Sections

Initially these small 'shock troops' were called the Special Duty Sections; but basically they were Commandoes in name.

Churchill said: "they must be prepared with specially trained troops of the hunter class who can develop a reign of terror down the enemy coast."

However, even as the first missions were planned, volunteers were being called for a new organization; the Commandoes. Men from the Independent Companies volunteered, making a new force; No 11 Independent Company.

Despite the recent retreat from France, Churchill threw this new force back at Hitler's coastal wall in their first raid, just 20 days after the end of Dunkirk.

### Operation Collar

On 24th June, 1940, four fast Royal Air Force air-sea rescue boats put the men ashore. Basically, the Commandoes walked around a bit, fired at a few Germans, and disembarked to come back home. An ignominious beginning, true, but at least not a disaster.

When the men returned from Operation Collar, the Commandoes became the official name for the new strike force.

By the Autumn of 1940, the Commandoes had over 2000 men under their command.

### Australian Commandoes

Incidentally Australia copied the formation of British Commandoes to the letter. In 1941/42, they coalesced their scattered and disorganized 'special forces' into Independent Companies. In mid 1943, with a reorganization of the whole Australian Army, these units were re-designated 'Commandoes'.

Commandoes prepare for operations behind enemy lines, D-day, 1944

**Final Version 3; The Commandoes**

After a memo by Dudley Clarke, the organization was quickly formed. Most of the units were British in origin, numbered No1 to No9 Commando. No 10 Commando was formed from soldiers from countries conquered by the Nazis. No 12 was Scottish, No 14 was Arctic trained.

There were 4 units deployed to the Middle East, No's 50, 51, 52 and Middle East 54 Commando.

62 Commando was a special raiding squadron known as the Small Scale Raiding Force, under direct control of the SOE, and No 2 Commando were trained as paratroopers.

Trained in the Scottish highlands, the rank and file were trained in unarmed combat, sniping, explosives and other facets of irregular warfare. They were the closest to guerillas that existed in the British Army.

The Commandoes performed in almost every theater of the war, earning battle honors far exceeding the normal units. They were involved in far too many operations to be listed here, in fact, it would probably be easier to list the operations they did *not* take part in.

**HMS Cambeltown, blown apart on the main locks of St Nazaire's dry dock. The dock, used for large battleships, was never used again**

Between 1940 and 1944, the Commandoes executed 36 raids on France, the most famous being the 1942 raid on St Nazaire, Operation Chariot where HMS Campbeltown was rammed directly into the Normandy dock gates. The Commandoes also took part in the Dieppe Raid in the same year.

**Commandoes returning from Dieppe. Despite the raid being a disaster, the Commandoes had mostly achieved their objectives**

They fought in the deserts of North Africa, and throughout the Italian campaign.

The fought on the Normandy beaches and behind enemy lines.

They fought in the jungles of Burma.

## Small Scale Raiding Force

The Small Scale Raiding Force (SSRF), also known as 62 Commando, worked directly under the SOE, and would be the precursor to SAS. Commanded by Louis Mountbatten, they performed many missions against German bases and shipping, both on mainland Europe, Africa and beyond.

When 62 Commando was broken up in 1943, members formed the Special Boat Section (SBS), and No2 SAS.

Specific SSRF operations are Postmaster, Savanna, Aquatint, Basalt, and Chestnut.

## The Commando Influence

Using the model of the British Commandos as an example, other countries soon formed their own elite squads.

### Canada

In 1942, a joint Canadian-American special forces unit was formed, the 1st Special Service Force, nicknamed the Devil's Brigade.

### Australia

The Australian Army formed their first commando units in 1942, initially known as the Australian Independent Companies.

### New Zealand

New Zealand formed their own guerillas in 1942, the Southern Independent Commando in Fiji 1942.

### France

Commandoes Marine are a French Special Forces unit formed in May 1942, landing on Normandy beaches on Sword Beach.

### Netherlands

The Korps Commandotroepen (KCT) are a Dutch commando unit, first formed in March 1942. They served in Sumatra, fighting the Japanese.

### Belgium

The Paracommando Brigade is the Belgian version of the British Commandoes, formed in 1942. It now is called the Immediate Reaction Cell, and comprises both Commando and SAS troops supported by artillery.

As a footnote, it could be argued by some that the Germans were the first country to form Commando units (although not actually 'called' Commandos).

In September 1939, Germans quickly infiltrated behind Polish lines and sabotaged key areas of their combat and communications infrastructure. Using these irregular units as a model, the German Office for Foreign and Counter-Intelligence, formed the Brandenburger Regiment. The full title was '800th Special Purpose Training and Construction Company'.

They were Commandos in all but name.

The most famous of all, (Otto Skorzeny) commanded many special operations directly under the thumb of Adolf Hitler, including rescuing Italian dictator Benito Mussolini.

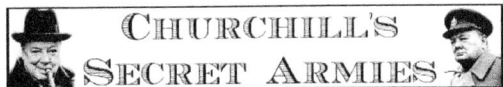

# THE MAUD COMMITTEE

Once again, and by now these revelations should be coming as no surprise at all, Churchill was at the spearhead of world leaders.

The MAUD Committee was formed by Winston Churchill in the early days of June, 1940, and named after an intriguing line (once thought to have been a code word) in a letter from Danish Physicist Niels Bohr. The committee was the direct result of a memorandum written by Rudolf Peierls (German Jew) and Otto Frisch (Austrian Jew), both working at Birmingham University in England. The memorandum explained their theoretical design for the detonation of an atomic bomb.

(Ultimately both Peierls and Frisch would join the Manhattan Project in the sands of new Mexico)

William Penney, Otto Frisch, Rudolf Peierls, and John Cockroft

Not wanting to keep all the eggs in the one basket, from June 1940, the MAUD committee used four universities as sites for theoretical and practical physics for the production of a nuclear weapon...

Birmingham University, led by Australian Mark Oliphant also included German refugees Rudolf Peierls, Otto Frisch and Klaus Fluchs and worked mostly in theory.

Liverpool University, led by Englishman and 1935 Nobel prize winner, James Chadwick, investigated thermal diffusion.

Oxford University, led by fleeing German-Jew, Franz Simon, inherited fleeing French physicists and the last Norwegian heavy water before the Nazi invasion.

Cambridge University, led by Professor Rideal, this included Swiss Egon Bretscher, Englishman Norman Feather, and investigated the uses of the newly discovered element, Plutonium. They also included French scientists and the French 'heavy water program'.

On July 15th, 1941, after a year of writing, the research finally culminated in two reports; 'Use of Uranium for a Bomb' and 'Use of Uranium as a source of power'. These two reports were known collectively as the MAUD report. The reports emphasized the necessity of a super-bomb in the Allied war effort.

Churchill, in his usual style decided that such a powerful secret department should have a wholly ambiguous name; hence the world's first nuclear program was officially named "Tube Alloys".

The "Tube Alloys" organization had particular ties to the growing British chemical conglomerate, Imperial Chemical Industries (ICI), and had experimental premises at one of their industrial premises.

The initial work was carried out in secret, and on 30th August, 1941, Winston Churchill officially authorized the research, and became the first world leader to authorize and approve a nuclear weapons program.

At this point, America was not at war, so Mark Oliphant flew to America with a copy of the reports, effectively setting up the groundwork of the Manhattan Project.

One report suggested that, although the initial prototypes could be built in England, the main production should be done in the safety of Canada.

At the end of 1942, because of the risk of spies and bombings, the complete cadre of scientists was relocated to the University of Montreal in Canada. By Spring 1943, the research team had grown to over 300 personnel.

The August 1943 Quebec Agreement between Britain, Canada and USA, stated clearly that all allies would share in any developments, and the Canadian scientists were sent to the purpose-built site in the deserts of Los Alamos, New Mexico.

Incidentally, a leaked two-year-old copy of the MAUD report was received by Stalin in 1943, who set up his own nuclear bomb program immediately.

The combination of minds produced the bomb in 1945, and two bombs were detonated in japan, bringing the war to a close.

Afterword... it must be said here, that the USA never divulged the details of the nuclear program to either the British or Canada.

(The USA cited the discovery of spy leaks to Stalin as the basis for their non-disclosure)

At the end of the war, after working together for two years, the British-based scientists were dismissed.

The British had to develop their own program, and in 1952 detonated their first bomb.

In 1958, the USA finally agreed to share nuclear technology with Britain again.

There you go... from Churchill's mouth to Hiroshima, in one short chapter.

# THE BUREAU CENTRAL DE RENSEIGNEMENTS ET D'ACTION (BCRA)

### Charles de Gaule

In the days after Dunkirk, as Churchill scrambled to grab control of the situation, many other politicians in power in London were in free-fall. It was a time of total functional instability, of desperate phone calls, families fleeing the city to relatives in the country.

In the center of the melee stood General Charles de Gaulle.

Charles de Gaule, self-proclaimed president of the Free French Forces

De Gaulle had been a Commander of one of the few French divisions that had fought well against the rapid German advance. His advancement was lightning fast...

17th May, Colonel de Gaulle's 200 tanks attacked the Germans at Montcornet.

24th May, he was promoted to Brigadier General.

28th May, he attacked the German forces around Dunkirk, trying to break through.

5th June, he was appointed as Under Secretary of State for National Defense and War, making him responsible for coordination with the British forces, most now safely arrived in Britain.

16th June, Marshal Pétain became Premier and planned to seek an armistice with Nazi Germany.

17th June, de Gaulle, with other senior officers, rebelled against the aims of the new French government; on the morning of 17 June, de Gaulle and a few senior French flew to Britain.

18th June, in a radio broadcast, authorized by Churchill himself, de Gaulle called for all Frenchmen to follow him.

General de Gaule in Paris, 1944

De Gaulle, by his radio announcement, and by being the senior officer to flee France had become the Premier of a new nation; the Free French.

When General de Gaulle broadcast, the Special Operations Executive (SOE) was only five days old; Britain's new counter-espionage master department into which every aspect of British Military Intelligence was to report to.

The Free French Government-in-exile, now located in London, was in worse condition than its biggest ally. The French Army was in tatters, most of its personnel captured, most of its armaments lost, its armor lost forever. The standing of the French Navy was in doubt, and to all purposes, the French Air Force no longer existed.

Free French forces were at their lowest ebb, and their intelligence network was in tatters.

**Thousands of French women joined the resistance. The BCRA, with the SOE, supplied arms, explosives and information**

# THE BUREAU CENTRAL DE RENSEIGNEMENTS ET D'ACTION (BCRA)

The Free French Government-in-exile needed an intelligence service of its own, and considering its country was surrendering to Germany, it needed one fast.

On the same day as his speech, de Gaulle, again with Churchill's permission, formed the Service de Renseignements (SR) or "Information Service" in English. The name would change again before settling on The Bureau Central De Renseignements Et D'action (BCRA) in 1942. It would eventually be re-branded as the SDECE after the war.

In 1940/41, as Frenchmen flocked to the Free-French cause, the BCRA grew, spawning many departments, a few of which I list below. (Thankfully my French is considerably better than my Polish)

**Action Militaire (A/M):** created 15 April 1941, working in close partnership with 'F' Section of the British Special Operations Executive.

**Contre-Espionnage (CE):** created 16 December 1941, working with the British MI5, the British 'Home' Intelligence Service.

**Évasion (E):** created February 1942, working with the newly formed British MI9, broken away from MI6 just three months earlier.

**Politique (N/M for non militaire):** August 1942.

**Renseignement (R):** which worked closely with British intelligence agencies MI(R) and MI6.

# THE SPECIAL BOAT SECTION (SBS)

After completing a Commando course in Scotland in the summer of 1940, Lieutenant Roger Courtney tried to convince Admiral of the Fleet Sir Roger Keyes Admiral Theodore Hallett, of the need for a covert navy special operations unit using folding kayaks. He was turned down at least once.

SBS used collapsible canoes, and trained to paddle for miles to the objective

Undaunted, days later he attempted to solo infiltrate HMS Glengyle, a Landing Ship full of infantry anchored in the River Clyde. Courtney paddled to the ship on his kayak, climbed aboard undetected, wrote his initials on the door to the captain's cabin, and stole a deck gun cover. On presentation of the wet cover to the Admirals, he was promoted to captain and given command of twelve men. He called them the Special Boat Section.

They soon increased in size and performed operations chiefly in the Mediterranean Sector, in Greece, Crete and in the Italian Campaign. At one point they were incorporated into the SAS, then broke away again.

They are still considered to be one of the top Special Forces Units in the world.

Commandoes walk past a collapsed boat, the kind used by the SBS

# CHURCHILL'S SECRET ARMIES

# THE BATTLE OF BRITAIN'S FIGHTER COMMAND

"Never in the field of human conflict, was so much owed by so many, to so few."

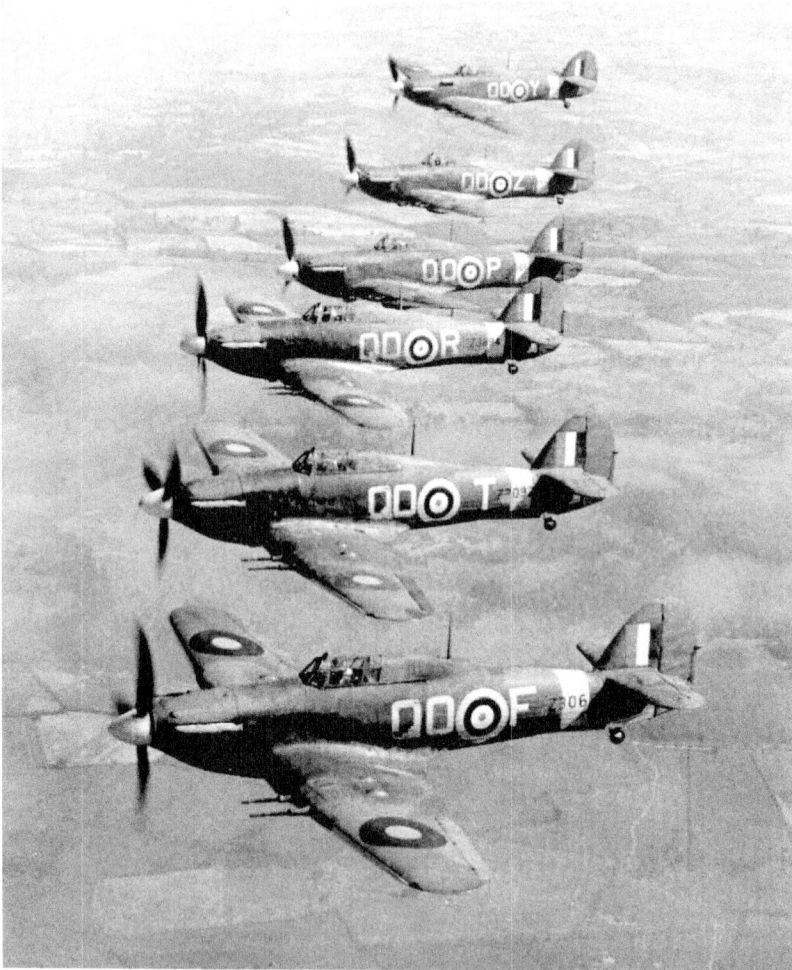

Considered Britain's 'ugly' fighter, more Hurricanes were built than Spitfires

Fighter Command was a command structure within the Royal Air Force (RAF) which controlled the operations and tactics of the fighter aircraft stationed in Britain. This 'internal structure' was to be the organizational miracle that kept the RAF flying during World War 2.

118

In March, 1935, flaunting the German dismissal of the Treaty of Versailles, Hitler revealed the new 'Luftwaffe', boasting that it was already stronger than the RAF.

As Germany planned for the war, between 1936 and 1939, Fighter Command gradually replaced the obsolete biplanes of the old war with revolutionary Hawker Hurricanes and Supermarine Spitfires. When Germany invaded Western Europe on 10th May, 1940, the fighter aircraft of the RAF had already flown against German fighters in Norway; they were well matched. However, considering the placement of the airfields and the flight over the channel, fighting time over Europe was short, sometimes as little as twenty minutes. Very soon, the few squadrons of Hurricanes stationed in France limped home.

Churchill, in his usual manner, launched the battle in his speeches.

"What General Weygand called the Battle of France is over. I expect that the Battle of Britain is about to begin."

**Supermarine Spitfire, considered by many to be the best fighter ever built**

Thankfully when Churchill's 'Battle of Britain' began, there were three distinct advantages on Britain's side.

RAF Fighter Command was already in place, operational, and ready to fight.

RADAR stations, a far better version than was being operated by the Germans, was already in place, supplying real-time images directly to Fighter Command.

German fighters flying time over England was as low as twenty minutes, before they had to return to France.

## FIGHTER COMMAND STRUCTURE

RAF Fighter Command Radar was not a complicated structure, in fact, it was kept to a basic level on purpose; the more complex the system, the more parts are available to make it fail.

Bentley Priory; Fighter Command sat in the very center of the building

### Bentley Priory

Bentley Priory was a converted girl's school housing the command center of military air defense in Britain (formally Air Defense of Great Britain (ADGB)).

Underground bunkers were built to house the operational centers, the main house was used for administration, lodgings, and the officer's quarters.

Situated in a large 90 acre estate on the north-west of London's suburbs, it was perfectly situated near to the capital, yet unassuming out in the country. The outside of the building was sprayed with brown and green paint. Considering its importance, it was only hit twice by bombs, causing little damage.

## The Filter Room

This was the main RAF Fighter Command operational center, rebuilt and strengthened deep in the depths of the large house. All messages from observers and all radar tracks were directed here, then distributed physically onto a huge map of southern England. Fighter Command officers would view the map from galleries above the main map board. It was a primitive system, yes, but easily understood and easy to see the large picture of any attack.

It must be remembered that many different raids from different Luftwaffe stations overlapped; the Luftwaffe raids were rarely organized into one large attack, rather they would stagger their attacks to increase pressure on British air crews and pilots.

It was necessary to follow each group of planes, and identify targets, numbers and types of aircraft, and to keep track of each group until they left British airspace.

The Filter room; Commanders would watch from numerous balconies

It must also be understood that Britain had too few fighters, pilots and fuel to keep a regularly staffed air patrol. Only when the German planes crossed a certain part of the channel, and their target and direction confirmed, could Fighter Command 'scramble' the proper squadrons closest to that flightpath. It was basically a game of chess, played with the highest stakes.

Observers on the ground relayed aircraft numbers & types to the Filter Room

### RADAR

Born in Brechin, Scotland, Robert Alexander Watson-Watt pioneered the development of radar in Britain. Watson-Watt was a direct descendant of James Watt, the famous Scottish engineer and inventor of the steam engine. Radar had been researched in many countries, but in 1936, Watson-Watt joined the Air Ministry, was paired with Arnold Watkins, and their work funded by the government was put into practical use. All along the east and south coasts of England aircraft detection and tracking stations were built, and antennae erected.

These stations were linked directly to Fighter Command at Priory House.

The system was not perfect, but it was better than any other in use at the time. Its range meant it could detect aircraft over the coast of France at the narrowest parts of the English Channel. At the shortest distance, travelling at 250 miles per hour (the speed of the bombers), they would arrive over the English coast in just ten minutes.

(Incidentally, Watson-Watt was reportedly pulled over for speeding in Canada after the war. His speed had been logged by a policeman armed with a radar gun. He wrote a poem 'Rough Justice' to commemorate the occasion;

Pity Sir Robert Watson-Watt, strange target of this radar plot
And thus, with others I can mention, the victim of his own invention.
His magical all-seeing eye, enabled cloud-bound planes to fly
But now by some ironic twist, it spots the speeding motorist
And bites, no doubt with legal wit, the hand that once created it.

Such wonderful irony.)

## Observation Corps

The radar readings were noted, and the Observation Corps alerted, men and women all over England, trained in aircraft recognition, who would confirm the sightings. When the Observation Corps had confirmed the radar sightings, details and numbers were added to the 'blocks' on the table of the Filter Room. Only then were decisions made on which squadrons would be scrambled.

Fighter Command then alerted the airfields, relaying the information it had. The radio operators at Fighter Command then guided the RAF fighters directly onto the enemy formations.

The system was very simple; but it worked.

## BATTLE OF BRITAIN

The Battle of Britain, coined by Winston Churchill on 18th June in parliament, is the term given to the Second World War defense of the United Kingdom by the RAF. In Britain, the officially recognized dates are 10th July to 31st October 1940, and is now considered the first properly defined 'air war' in history.

(It is not to be confused with the 'Blitz'; the term given to the period of large-scale night attacks against London. The Blitz is widely accepted as starting on 7th September 1940 and ending on 21st May 1941. In all, 16 British cities suffered air raids with at least 100 tons of high explosives. In 267 days, London was attacked 71 times,

Birmingham, Liverpool and Plymouth 8 times, Bristol 6, Glasgow 5, Southampton 4, Portsmouth 3, and Hull 3.)

As Hitler considered an Invasion of Britain, he reasoned that without full control of the skies above his landing sites, the mission would fail. Goering, chief of the Luftwaffe, took up the challenge, saying he would destroy the RAF.

Hurricane pilots in good spirits; pilots could be asked to fly 5 sorties per day

### The Pilots

German pilots had honed their skills in the Spanish Civil war, and again over the skies of Poland. British pilots were on the whole less experienced, some fresh from training with few hours in the air.

The Luftwaffe attacked airfields and RAF installations daily, sometimes more than once. Day by day, as the pilots became tired, the losses climbed. A call was given to the recruiters, calling on new pilots, and soon the ranks were swelled by foreign pilots.

The lists from the time give the pilots nationalities as below.

Out of a total of 2,936 pilots on the RAF lists, 595 were not British...

145 Poles, 127 New Zealanders, 112 Canadians, 88 Czechoslovaks, 10 Irish, 32 Australians, 28 Belgians, 25 South Africans, 13 French, 7

Americans, 3 Southern Rhodesians and one each from Jamaica and Palestine.

The pilots could have not have come at a better time, with the planes evenly matched. It would soon come down to a matter of attrition.

The Polish pilots were the most sought after, they had fought against Luftwaffe, albeit just for a month.

With multiple raids per day, getting the pilots re-fueled and back in the air was of particular importance. According to RAF figures, the record for a fighter squadron to land, turn, get refueled, rearmed, and take off was just SEVEN minutes. For a whole squadron.

On 12th August, Goering launched increased attacks, his main assault being on RADAR installations and forward airfields. The sorties increased, the casualties built up.

Luftwaffe Head, Hermann Goering (right) always had a 'stupid' smug smile on his face, even as he faced the death penalty at Nuremburg

Three days later, Goering launched 'Eagle day'; a concerted attack to finally stop the RAF. In one massive attack, the Luftwaffe flew 1500 sorties; they lost 45 planes to the RAF's 13. The numbers were turning, but the RAF were putting fewer and fewer planes into the air every single day.

Again Goering tried a concentrated attack. On the 18th the Germans came again, this time the crucial targets were big hits on command and control stations. In a single day the Luftwaffe lost 71planes to the RAF's 34.

Every single day of the summer, the skies above southern England were full of white trails. The men from both sides were constantly in action, and although the British were always outnumbered, they always downed more German planes than they lost.

RAF pilots scramble to their Spitfires. Note the mascot dog, joining the charge

But now the men were beyond exhaustion, the planes needed attention, the leaders accepted their precious RAF Fighter Command was at breaking point.

On 20th August, a mistake happened that changed the battle. The Germans, during a night raid, lost their way, and bombed the outskirts of London.

The people were up in arms, parliament reacted, and Churchill ordered a retaliatory strike against Berlin.

Hitler was outraged, considering he'd stated on many occasions that bombs would never fall on German cities, and swung the focus of the German bombers to London instead of the beleaguered airfields.

The War Office thought the change of plans announced the start of the German invasion. Sirens sounded, and the code word 'CROMWELL' was broadcast on the BBC, the signal for the Auxiliary Units to take to ground.

The fighter pilots, not being bombed themselves, flew fewer sorties, now being directed only against the bombers over London. This short respite gave the airfields what they needed; time to rebuild.

On 15th Sept, Goering launched a huge attack on London, trying to tease the RAF into the air, to 'finally' destroy the RAF. At one point during the raid, every fighter in Fighter Command was in the sky. The Luftwaffe lost sixty planes to the RAF's 30.

Two days later, Hitler ordered a postponement to Operation Sealion, their plan to invade.

Fighter Command had won the battle of Britain.

RAF pilots scramble to Hurricanes, their ground crews already waiting

# THE COMBINED OPERATIONS HEADQUARTERS

With the country still reeling from Dunkirk, and the first 'Commando' raid (Operation Collar on 23 June 1940) being a non-event, Churchill realized the need for a new level of inter-departmental cooperation on small scale actions. The only way to do this was set up a new inter-force command unit, a buffer between the services, and give it a commander of some hubris; someone whose orders would be obeyed without the usual inter-service wrangling.

Admiral-of-the-Fleet Roger Keyes was the first director, from July 1940 to October 1941, when he was replaced by Lord Louis Mountbatten.

**Lord Louis Mountbatten was universally popular; killed by IRA bomb in 1979**

Combined Operations Headquarters (COH) was the first 'joint-operations' organizational department of the British War Office. First set up as an individual head of a chain of command, it gradually became the go-to place for new ideas, or where a special liaison was required.

The department was staffed by thinkers, whose job was to plan operations and to develop ideas and inventions to harass the enemy in any way possible.

## Combined Operations Pilotage Parties

Combined Operations Headquarters covered all those who worked with landing craft, a rough but reliable method of getting a small force to a beach and away again. Most landing craft could cope with medium seas, yet land a force in just two feet of water. The badge of Combined Operations was an eagle over a submachine gun over an anchor, reflecting the three service arms; the Royal Air Force, the British Army and the Royal Navy.

Among the projects undertaken by Combined Operations was the surveying of landing sites for invasions, including those of Sicily and Normandy (a later chapter). These were carried out by Combined Operations Pilotage Parties made up of members of the Royal Navy, Royal Marines, Corps of Royal Engineers and Special Boat Service.

## COH Missions

These took many forms, and although only a few were absolutely just COH operations, most other raiding operations had the hand of the COH in them somewhere. These are a selection of the more famous involvements, showing the diversity of the department's immersion...

The German radar station, near Bruneval, France

**Operation Biting**; also called the 'Raid on Bruneval' in France, 1942. British bombers were getting hit by fighters much quicker, and the RAF suspected a new radar system (The Würzburg radar). Special Forces were parachuted near the radar base, where, after a short fire-fight, RAF scientists/technicians with the force dismantled vital parts of the radar array. They then took the pieces to the nearby coast where they were taken aboard by NAVY/SBS/Marines landing craft. Since speed was of the essence, they were then transferred to Motor Gun Boats, and quickly taken back to Britain. This was a typical involvement of the COH, utilizing many different aspects of the British Armed Forces.

**Operation Frankton**; called the "Cockleshell heroes", this was a Commando canoe attack, launched from a submarine offshore, on French shipping in Bordeaux. Six ships were damaged in the raid. Churchill rather optimistically said that this one raid had shortened the war by six months.

**The Mulberry Harbors**; the Combined Operations Headquarters were heavily involved in the inter-departmental development of the portable harbors for D-Day.

Mulberry Harbor; Floating sections for ships to unload, and the roadways (left) going off to the shore

**Project Habakkuk**; a plan to build huge aircraft carriers from a mix of sawdust and ice, called pykrete. This idea got as high up the tree as you can climb. In a meeting with Churchill and his admirals, Mountbatten entered the room with two blocks and placed them on a table; one a normal ice block, the other pykrete. He then shot at the ice block. It shattered to pieces. He then fired at the pykrete; the bullet ricocheted off the block, grazing the trouser leg of Admiral Ernest King, and got embedded in the wall.

X-Class submarine, like the ones used in Operation Gambit to mark the British/Canadian Normandy beaches

**Operation Gambit**; two small X-class submarines were used on D-Day to clearly mark the limit of the British/Canadian Sword and Juno beaches. The submarines arrived on the 4th June, and stayed submerged until the 6th, when they surfaced, and erected the transmitting device and a large light shining seaward at each edge. The same service was offered to the Americans at Omaha and Utah; the declined the offer.

**Operation Cockade**; was a triple deception by the LCS and Ops (B), two deception departments, to draw German troops away from Italy (and therefore stationed elsewhere) for the Sicily landings. The deceptions were to be backed up by double agents, decoy radio signals, fake troop concentrations, commando raids, and increased reconnaissance and bombing missions into the areas of Boulogne, Brest and Norway. First, they threatened an invasion of Norway from imaginary forces in Scotland. This would be 'cancelled', and the Allied resources pushed to an amphibious landing in France.

Whilst Hitler did not completely fall for the ruse, an additional 50,000 German troops were sent to Norway.

**Footnote to Operation Cockade**

If anything good had come of Operation Cockade, it was this; the misinformation caused the German High Command to believe the Allies had 55 divisions in Britain, when they only had 17.

Hitler, using the deception data, became convinced of the existence of Operation Cockade's "First United States Army Group (FUSAG)". The 'existence' of this fictitious army group, and the gravitas of its commander, General Patton, made Hitler delay sending troops to Normandy Beaches on D-day, believing that the main attack was still to come.

American troops land on Slapton Sands, during Operation Tiger

**Operation Tiger**; a practice at D-Day, on April, 1944, at Slapton Sands, Devon. 30,000 American soldiers and a full fleet of landing craft and support ships took part. Firstly, a late change in plans caused a live naval bombardment to clash with American troops landing. The fleet was then attacked by German E-boats, (fast torpedo boats) and landing craft hit. Over 700 American men died on that exercise. However, crucial mistakes were rectified in time for Operation Overlord, ten weeks later.

**Operation Pluto**; this was the construction and laying of fuel delivery pipelines from Britain to France, (full chapter later).

Operation Pluto; thousands of miles of pipeline wait to be joined into 80 mile sections

# THE CICHOCIEMNI (SILENT UNSEEN)

Members of the 'Silent Unseen', Kedyw Unit, Home Army, 1944

(I believe it is pronounced Chick-Chemni)

On September 20th, 1940, the Cichociemni (Silent Unseen) were officially formed as an elite special-operations division of the Polish Army, then in exile in Britain. They trained with the SOE and completed the same commando training schools as the British Commandoes. Skilled in every facet of modern irregular warfare, they were soon ready to be inserted behind enemy lines in Poland.

Poland was the fourth biggest Allied Army in World War 2, and was sometimes forgotten in the histories of the period. However regular Polish troops in the Allied army fought well, and won many battle honors, including the Battle of Monte Cassino in Operation Diadem. Polish pilots also played a huge part in the Battle of Britain and further air operations. In 1940, (as shown in the last chapter) they were the largest non-British contingent of pilots In the RAF. No. 10 Commando was also the biggest Commando Unit, and was formed mostly from the poles of No. 1 Independent Company.

But this is the story of one man's dream.

## Captain Jan Górski

After the German invasion of Poland, Jan Górski escaped to France, and as the Germans prepared to invade his new country, he wrote a report for the Polish Chief of Staff. In the report, Górski proposed creation of a clandestine force to maintain contact with the Polish underground Związek Walki Zbrojnej (ZWZ, or Union of Armed Struggle). Górski submitted the report several times with no affirmative action taken.

Then the Germans invaded France, and Górski and his close cadre made their way to England. Not to be diverted from his idea, Górski took example from German paratroops used in Poland, and drafted another report, this time advocating a Polish airborne force, trained as Commandoes, to be used to support covert operations. Again, the plan was not received. But someone had been listening.

At the time of writing, I cannot determine the fate of Captain Jan Górski, but he may have survived both the Warsaw Uprising and the war, dying in 1963.

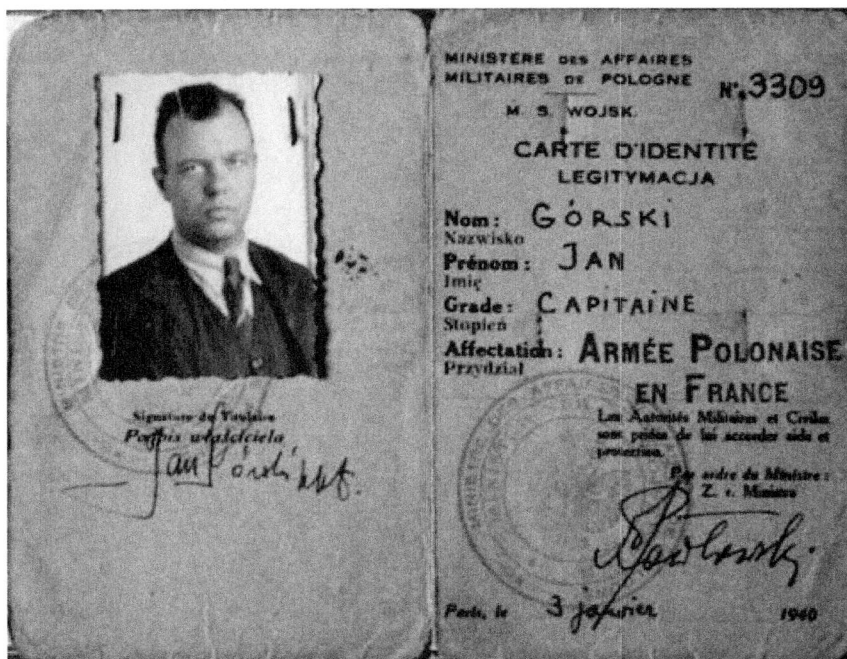

The ID card of Jan Gorski, issued 3rd January, 1940, before the fall of France

## Section III

Finally on 20th September, 1940, the Polish commander-in-chief called for the creation of such a unit. Section III would be trained in SOE schools, and made ready for covert operations in Poland, including insertion, partisan support and leadership, and air delivery of arms and supplies.

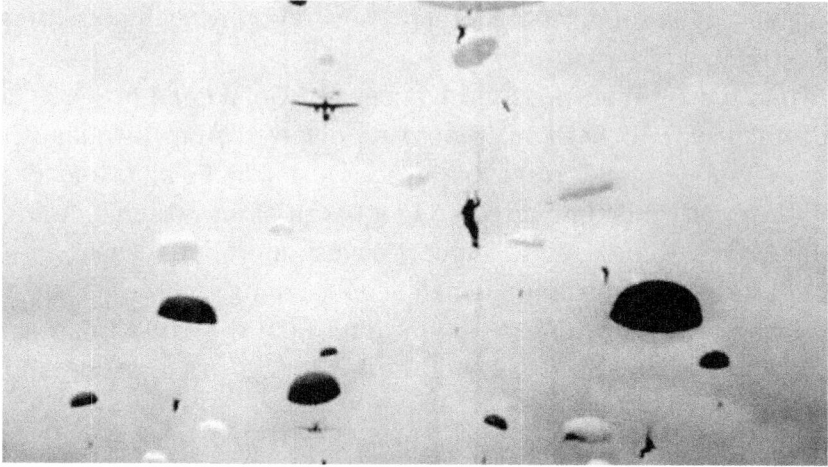

Cichociemni, parachuting into Poland

Since September 1939, various resistance and partisan groups had risen, schizmed by political faction, these groups rarely worked together...

**The Armia Krajowa (Home Army).** Incorporating the ZWZ, at their height may have numbered 400,000 or more. Not only did they sabotage and fight small forces, they also had the strength and support to take on full-size German troop numbers.

**Związek Walki Zbrojnej (ZWZ, or Union of Armed Struggle).** They fought from the inception of German rule, combining themselves with the Armia Krajowa (Home Army), in 1942. It is thought they numbered 250,000.

**Narodowa Organizacja Wojskowa (National Military Organization, NOW).** Created in October 1939, it did not merge with the Service for Poland's Victory (SZP), Union of Armed Struggle (ZWZ), or later Home

Army (AK). It did recognize the Polish government in exile in London, and is known to have had 80,000 plus members.

**Narodowe Siły Zbrojne (English National Armed Forces, NSZ).** An anti-Nazi and anti-Soviet military organization, the NSZ was right-wing, anti-Semite and accused of killing Jews during and after the war. They numbered up to 75,000 at their height.

**The Pomeranian Griffin.** Operating in Prussia and Pomerania, this group may have numbered 20,000.

**The Konfederacja Narodu (Confederation of the Nation)** was the resistance movement of a far-right political group, and never achieved great numbers.

It was time to both utilize and support these independent organisations; Section lll were seen as the solution.

Members of the Chicociemni, receiving medals for bravery after the war

### Cichociemni ("Silent Unseen")

The origins of the name have as many differing anecdotal origins as the Polish groups above. Basically, it may never be known for any certainty. One thread is recurring... "Silent Unseen" may have a connection with soldiers disappearing from regular Polish Army positions to volunteer for the new SOE driven units.

Under supervision of the SOE (but not under their direct orders), the Polish section of the SOE began to recruit members for their new force.

Officers and ranks of the Cichociemni, proudly wearing their full dress ribbons

When the group had chosen its first group, they were sent to Scotland to be trained in SOE and Commando camps. Many more groups were to follow. These schools were in 5 distinct areas of operation, and I apologize in advance for my bad Polish.

**Physical-conditioning (zaprawowy).** Held in the Commando camps and SOE camps in Scotland. Taught in the use of foreign weapons, and in mine and explosive deployment.

**Psychological and technical (badań psychotechnicznych).** Also held in the STS camps in Scotland. Taught basic covert operations, self-defense, silent killing, topography, cryptography, and sharpshooting.

**Parachuting (spadochronowy).** Held in Ridgeway Airfield, near Manchester.

**Covert-operations (walki konspiracyjnej).** Probably held in Audley End House, Essex. Taught the new way of life in occupied Poland, German-imposed laws, current fashions.

**Finals (odprawowy).** Held in the SOE finishing schools near London. Taught all aspects of their new identities, including evasion, lying, and resisting torture.

**Cichociemni, at parachute training; RAF Ridgeway, Manchester**

According to official figures, of the 2,413 candidates who were recruited, only 605 managed to complete both the physical and technical training. Of those, only 579 qualified for action in Poland. All who passed the training were initiated into the Home Army.

Once airlifted into Poland, Silent Unseen depending on their political persuasion agents were assigned to the ZWZ and Home Army, and other units. Many rose to become important cogs in the Polish resistance movement.

The Polish resistance movements kept hundreds of thousands of Germans occupied, keeping many divisions away from the front lines.

# THE NORWEGIAN INDEPENDENT COMPANY 1

Norwegian Independent Company; parachute training at RAF Ridgeway

### THE GERMAN INVASION

Geographically, the German invasion of Norway was a terrific physical challenge, and because of its rugged coast and mountainous countryside, holding onto and patrolling the captured ground without committing vast numbers of troops would be difficult. But the invasion was a primary objective for Hitler and his Third Reich, and he had many reasons behind his tactics.

### Iron Ore

Because of the Baltic Sea's capacity to freeze in winter, Sweden's vast iron ores had to be transported by rail across to Norway to Narvik, on the North Sea. Germany needed this ore to drive the industry of the war, and this was their primary concern.

### Nuclear Weapons

As early as 1934, there was a drive amongst scientists all over the world to develop a new technology, to harness nuclear energy. There was no doubt in the high echelons of the world's scientists and politicians that the first country to break through the basics of the fledgling science, and convert the energy into a weapon would win the war. For the research and production of such technology, the scientists needed heavy water ($H_3O$), one of the by-products of hydroelectricity, and the Norwegians were at the forefront of hydro-electric energy production.

**Oil Production**

Fish oils were a huge industry in Northern Norway, and these oils were considered precious to the Germans, considering they had little natural oil in their own countries. (The rich oil fields of the Ukraine were one of the reasons Hitler invaded Russia).

**A Base for Atlantic Raids**

The rugged coast of Norway was a hiding place for the ships of the *Reichsmarine*, the German Navy, and a perfect place to raid the North Atlantic. Hitler knew that the Royal Navy could blockade Germany as a sea power; owning Norway would diminish that threat.

**OPERATION WESERÜBUNG: GERMANY INVADES**

In 1939, as British, French and Belgian troops stood in France, awaiting Hitler's attack, Britain and France also sent troops to Norway, to reinforce their military strength, to cement their alliance, and to defend Sweden's iron ore route.

On 9th April, 1940, Germany invaded both Denmark and Norway. Hitler made a great show of his invasion of Norway being a reaction to the 'unfriendly Franco-British occupation'. He seemed to forget the allies were going to be fighting with the Norwegian Army.

Using similar Blitzkrieg tactics, even with Britain and France's support, the war against Norway lasted little more than two months.

It must be remembered, however, that the Norwegians lasted longer against the Nazi's invasion than any other European country. Both Poland and France surrendered after no more than a single month's fighting.

The Germans paid an expensive price for the capture of Norway; one that Hitler could not possibly have foreseen. The RAF and the Royal Navy fought against the German Navy, sinking two cruisers, three light cruisers and many other vessels; in all, ten percent of Hitler's Navy was lost.

A huge loss, from which the Kriegsmarine would never recover.

As the British disembarked, leaving Norway, they took with them some personnel from the Norwegian Army. After the surrender of France, Britain became the nucleus of the growing Norwegian resistance.

## The 'War' Against Norway

Apart from the disruption of economic supplies to Germany, Britain had many distinct reasons to keep up attacks on the Germans in Norway, and bolster any resistance in Norway.

The fjords, with their steep mountainous sides, are the perfect place to hide ships, and ideal locations to raid both the Atlantic, and any convoys bound for Russia. The RAF could not possibly keep tracks on all German naval deployment. The Norwegian Resistance, however, were constantly updating such movements, and alerted Britain of any of Germany's ships in local waters. The Tirpitz, Germany's flagship, and hope for Atlantic naval domination, was sunk in a Norwegian fjord by the bombs of the RAF.

Hitler had a constant fear of his empire being invaded, even from an early stage. Of all of the German conquests, Norway was the one far-flung cog in the Nazi wheel. Geographically cut off from Hitler's mainland Europe, it disproportionately required far more troops to occupy than any other single country. Every time the allies threatened to invade, Hitler reinforced. By the end of the war, Hitler had 350,000 men tied up in the occupation of Norway, at least 250,000 more than were required for such a task. If those extra 250,000 men could have been available at the battle of the Bulge, for instance, what a difference it would have made.

## NORWEGIAN HEROES

Many Norwegian men and women fought bravely against the Nazi yoke, the Norwegian Independent Company was awarded more medals man-for-man than most other units. But two must be mentioned by name...

## MARTIN LINGE

It is impossible to even mention the Norwegian Independent Company without the inclusion of a short history of Norwegian actor, Martin Linge.

When the Germans invaded Norway, 45 year-old Linge (as a reserve Lieutenant) joined his unit, and immediately became a liaison between the British and the Norwegian units. The first wounded Norwegian to be transported to Britain, he campaigned for a wholly Norwegian Unit to raid the Norwegian coast, saying; "Our land is perfect for secret resistance and guerrilla warfare".

Martin Linge, in Norwegian Army uniform, circa 1940

The SOE listened, and set him to gather and recruit like-minded Norwegians for such a task. Linge was a charismatic man, and after only 2 operations with his company, died in Norway in December 1941 in Operation Archery. His men subsequently called their company; *Kompani Linge* (or *Lingekompani*) in his honor.

Max Manus (right) as Crown Prince Olaf's personal bodyguard

## MAX MANUS

Maximo Guillermo Manus was one of the most famous saboteurs of World War 2. After fighting in the Finnish war, he was an originator of the Norwegian resistance movement and tried to assassinate Himmler and Goebbels on a visit to Oslo. He was arrested by the Gestapo in 1941, but escaped (via Sweden, Russia and Turkey) to Britain, where he joined the Norwegian Independent Company 1 (*Lingekompani*).

He became a specialist in ship sabotage and, by using Limpet mines, sank ships including the SS Donau, carrying troops to Germany, on 16 January 1945.

### Norwegian Independent Company 1

On March 1941, the SOE, realizing the growing group of Norwegians already wanting to 'get back in the war', formed Norwegian Independent Company 1. With their training based on both an elite commando-style, and Arctic training, the men were instantly put into action.

In Operation Claymore the Norwegian Independent Company landed with British Commandoes in the Lofoten islands in Northern Norway, blowing up crucial fish oil and glycerin production plants.

Operation Archery was a raid on Maloy, again destroying fish oil facilities and German shipping interests.

144

Disrupting Sweden's iron ore transportation was a primary military goal. The Thamshavn railway line between the iron ore mines and the sea was attacked four times, halting production and transportation of the ore.

Vermork Hydro-Electric plant at Rjukan, Norway. Heavy water was a by-product

### The Heavy Water Raids

The most famous of the Norwegian raids was undoubtedly the combination of Operations Grouse, Freshman, and Gunnerside; the disruption of Heavy water production at Vermork, Norway.

**Operation Grouse** was the first phase; the covert observation of the Vermork hydro-electric plant ay Rjukan. SOE trained locals surveyed the plant in October 1942, reporting back to Britain by radio.

**Operation Freshman**, a month later, was the first attempt to destroy the plant. Unfortunately, the attack never got started, one plane crashing, and the other detachment of paratroopers all being caught by the Gestapo and shot.

**Operation Gunnerside** was a success. A team of Norwegian Independent Company Commandoes raided the hydro-electric plant, blowing up the heavy water production area. On the facility being rebuilt, USA bombers raided the area, causing some damage. These raids caused the Germans to lose interest in such a remote facility, and move production of heavy water to Germany; fortunately this plan never reached the stage where the Germans could produce any usable material. In retrospect, Operation Gunnerside was possibly the most successful act of sabotage in all of the war.

Rjukan Hydro plant, showing the piping clearly. Even American bombing raids failed to stop Heavy water production

### The Bombing of the Hydro Ferry

Sustained bombings of the plant and the geographical remoteness forced the Germans into a difficult decision; they would have to move heavy water production to a closer, safer site.

The Germans ordered the remaining stocks of heavy water moved to Germany in bulk, where they would now manufacture themselves. The only route from the plant was by train, then over Lake Tinnsjo by ferry (a combined freight/passenger ship).

The Norwegian resistance knew that the transfer must be stopped at all costs; it made sense to blow up the ferry, with the heavy water onboard.

Charges were set aboard the ferry, timed to explode once the ship had reached a deep part of the lake. The operation was a complete success, although no one knew exactly how much heavy water had been destroyed.

Norwegian civilians were killed in the sinking, considered then to be a necessary consequence.

**The ferry across Lake Tinnsjo; the Germans loaded railcars of heavy water**

The actions are recounted in the Kirk Douglas movie, The *Heroes of Telemark*, and the Norwegian television series *The Heavy Water War*.

# THE ADVANCED HEADQUARTERS 'A' FORCE

### THE OVERVIEW

On 10th June 1940, exactly one month after Germany invaded France, Italy declared war on the Allies. The British (Middle East Command) forces in Egypt, collectively called the Eighth Army were commanded by General Archibald Wavell, a veteran of the First World war, and career soldier. Initially the British fought a defensive war against the outnumbering Italian for several months before striking back on 9th December.

Wavell's force of 30,000 men faced Italian troops numbering 150,000.

For his forward strike to take the Italians by surprise, he decided to deceive the Italians into thinking they were being attacked by a far larger force. Using dummy tanks, and false radio communications, Operation Compass was a total success, much of which Wavell attributed to the deception part of the operation.

An inflatable tank; deception was a new weapon in the war against the Nazis

The three months of Operation Compass captured 138,000 Italian prisoners, 400 tanks and 845 guns. It was a crushing blow for the Italian Army from which they never recovered; technically the Italian Army was out of the war.

On 13<sup>th</sup> December Wavell sent a communication to London, informing the War Office of his intention to use such tactics again, and his plan to form a separate department within his command to create and manage the deception.

The victory left a sour taste in the mouths of many; Wavell's victory had been so decisive, in February 1941, Field Marshall Rommel (to be known as the 'desert fox') was dispatched to command Germany's Afrika Korps.

A wooden framework could be covered by a tarpaulin and made to look like a camouflaged Churchill tank

### THE MAN BEHIND THE VISION

Despite joining the Army in time to fight in World War One, Dudley Clarke missed out and soon settled down to a life in desert postings, first in Mesopotamia in 1919, then Iraq the next year. He was on leave in Turkey in 1922, when he was caught up in the Chanak Crisis, where Turkish troops threatened to attack British and French. Clarke was given the job of feeding false information to Turkish, and his career in deception began.

Clarke was in London, trying to find support for the idea of a small strike force; his notion landed in many ears, and soon the Commandoes were born. Leaving the Commandoes in their infancy, Clarke received General Wavell's summons, and set off for Cairo, arriving on 18th December. His new title would be "Intelligence Officer (special duties) to the Commander in Chief".

An inflatable truck; inexpensive to manufacture, and quickly assembled

Using the cover of running a regional MI9 department (MI9 was responsible for training Allied servicemen in escape and evasion tactics, and providing them with help and assistance in getting back home), Clarke set to work in the British Army headquarters, Cairo.

Operation Abeam was an attempt to invent a fictional paratrooper regiment in Cairo, which Clarke called the 1st Special Air Service Brigade. This was to threaten the Italians with being hit behind the lines by paratroopers. After a successful deception against the Greek island of Rhodes, he began to recruit members to his staff.

In March 1941, Advanced Headquarters 'A' Force was officially born.

Ultimately 'A' Force's work in the desert came to the notice of the War Office, and Clarke was temporarily recalled to London, in late September 1941, to brief Churchill's Joint Planning Staff.

After hearing Clarke's presentation, they recommended to the Chiefs of Staff Committee that a similar department should be formed in London to spread the new art of deception across all theatres of war.

Advanced Headquarters 'A' Force ('A' Force) in Cairo ultimately became The London Controlling Section (LCS) and spawned Ops (B)

Nothing new under the sun; turns out deception was not an absolutely 'new' art. A confederate soldier standing next to some painted logs

# THE SPECIAL AIR SERVICE (SAS)

In July, 1941, using a name once fabricated by Dudley Clarke, the official Special Air Service (SAS) was formed. It is one of the most highly trained 'Elite Units' in the world, and is seen as the father and founder of them all.

It started as a single unit of 5 officers and 60 men, (Possibly by a single transfer from No 1 Special Boat Section) and by 1944, the had grown to brigade size, (5000 strong) incorporating both French and Belgian troops.

David Stirling has already been mentioned as the originator of the Long Range Desert Group, and the SAS were to be an offshoot of that unit.

**The SAS; unconventional mavericks who singlehandedly changed the war**

As part of a desert deception, Clarke and Stirling needed the Germans/Italians to believe that a complete paratrooper regiment was stationed in Libya/Egypt. They named this fictional unit; The Special Air Service.

To complement the LRDG's fast actions, Clarke also wanted a strike force to accompany some of the raids. The SAS (proper this time) was born, but called "L Detachment".

Their first Operation was a disaster, but their second, a night attack on German airfields, left 60 German planes destroyed for the loss of three men. Miraculous indeed.

In September 1942 the unit was renamed 1st SAS, and by that time the unit had already grown in size to four British squadrons, one Free French, one Greek, and the attached Folboat Section (another name for the Special Boat Section, the originator of all Navy Seals).

No 1 SAS were soon re-named the Special Raiding Section, another small secret army.

In 1944 the Brigade size SAS was formed as follows; British 1$^{st}$ SAS, British 2$^{nd}$ SAS, French 3$^{rd}$ SAS, French 4$^{th}$ SAS, and the Belgian 5$^{th}$ SAS.

Now posted to the main theatre of the European war, SAS Brigade was tasked with parachute operations behind the German lines in France, Belgium, the Netherlands (Operation Pegasus), and into Germany (Operation Archway).

The SAS; emulated but never equaled; the model for the world's elite forces

### Hitler's Commando Order

As a result of Hitler's issuing of the Commando Order, on 18$^{th}$ October 1942, SAS Brigade faced the additional danger of being summarily executed if ever captured by the Germans.

This only happened twice to the SAS.

In Operation Bulbasket, July 1944, 34 captured SAS commandos were executed by German troops, and in Operation Loyton, October 1944, 31 captured SAS commandos were also executed.

# THE POLITICAL WELFARE EXECUTIVE (PWE)

In Aug 1941, as SOE became cumbersome due to both its increased ranks and its increased workload, SOE1 (SOE's propaganda wing) became its own entity.

Now called the Political Welfare Executive (PWE), it was charged with producing and disseminating all white (anti-Nazi), black (pro-Nazi), and grey (non-political) propaganda, against the axis forces. Their main aim was twofold; to damage enemy morale and sustain and boost the morale of both the British/Allied populations, and those of the occupied countries.

Reporting directly to the Foreign Office, the initial staff came almost exclusively from SO1.

The Political Welfare Executive was different from most of Churchill's secret armies in that it was governed and overseen by a non-military committee of top level civil servants responsible only to Churchill himself.

Anthony Eden (Foreign Secretary), Brendan Bracken (Minister of Information) and Hugh Dalton (Minister of Economic Warfare), were the main talking heads of the PWE, and being civilians, they staffed and operated the unit differently from the norm.

From the outset the PWE included staff members from the Ministry of Information, the aforementioned propaganda elements of the SOE, and from the staff and directors of the BBC, who would broadcast their political messages. The main headquarters was Woburn Abbey (a large country mansion in Bedfordshire) with London offices at the BBC's Bush House.

The PWE were a gatherer of the truth from all over Europe. They used first-hand knowledge and rumor equally, gathering all kinds of information about real-time life in Germany and the occupied countries. Newspapers were gathered and read, escaped POW's and returned RAF crewmen told their stories.

Information is power, and the PWE used it to great effect, turning the smallest detail into a barb to spike their messages.

Sefton Delmer broadcasts the PWE messages throughout Europe

Propaganda was delivered in many forms.

Domestic Radio Broadcasts were used to deliver the news (what could be shared) and encourage civilians to succumb to the Government drives and initiatives. "Loose Lips Sink Ships, Dig For Victory, Saucepans For Spitfires, and many other messages brought the need for the civilian to play his or her part, no matter how small.

European Radio Broadcasts in English, French, Czech and Polish contained welcome good news for the occupied countries. Purposefully fake messages diverted German ears while messages to SOE and other European behind-the-lines units were broadcast. Anti-Nazi messages and advertisements carried terrible stories of life on the fighting front and of dirty tricks back home.

Postcards, leaflets and documents were dropped into both German field units and to the German civilian peoples. The civilians were told of horrible conditions on the front lines, and of the atrocities done by Germans and against them. Letters dropped to the soldiers told of men back home, consorting with their wives and girlfriends.

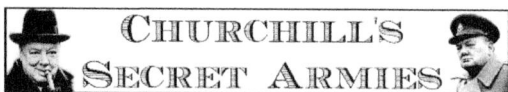

# THE LONDON CONTROLLING SECTION (LCS) INCLUDING OPS (B)

To find the absolute beginnings of this organization is difficult; the players and events are fluid. However, I see the London Controlling Section as a merging of two great players in the deception game.

Members of the London Controlling Section, in their 'war room', 1943

**Writer Dennis Wheatley** was recruited in 1941 to become the sole civilian in Churchill's bunker on the Joint Planning Staff. Tina Rosenberg wrote: "He went from writing for an audience of millions to writing for just 12 people but that dozen included the prime minister, the King and the heads of the armed services. And his fiction was this time aimed not at millions of readers but at only one – Adolf Hitler."

In what was a new and inexact science, Wheatley had a major say in most of the deception coming out of the War Office in the early days of the war. Operation Hardboiled was the biggest to come out of Wheatley's department in its early days. Hardboiled was the War Office's attempt to deceive Hitler that Britain was going to invade

Norway. Whatley set to work, interviewing Norwegians about landing sites and possible airfields; Hitler, always paranoid about Norway's safety, sent an extra 50,000 troops to support the 100,000 already there. Although the deception had been nowhere near perfectly executed, it laid the tracks for future works, and took an extra 50,000 Germans effectively out of the war.

**Brigadier Dudley Clarke**, working in Cairo, Egypt, during the first months of 1941, created what he called order-of-battle deceptions in the North African campaign. Under the name, Advanced Headquarters 'A' Force, Clarke had been working unofficially for months in the desert campaign; this was the first official section of Military Intelligence to be formed with the single purpose of deceiving the enemy.

Using radio broadcasts, dummy tanks, and using double agents to spread the lies, Clarke made the Germans believe that Allied military forces in the desert were far larger than reality. He invented entire divisions and armies, and German agents reported the movements of these fictional forces back to Hitler. By the spring of 1944, the Germans were convinced that the Allies had 14 divisions in Egypt and Libya. In fact there were little more than three, none of them battle-ready.

Deception in the desert; inside this harmless truck lurks a Churchill tank

'A' Force's work in the desert soon came to the notice of the War Office, and Clarke was recalled to London, in late September 1941, to brief Churchill's Joint Planning Staff.

After hearing Clarke's presentation, they recommended to the Chiefs of Staff Committee that a similar department should be formed in London to spread the new art of deception across all theatres of the war.

Called the London Controlling Section (LCS), just to keep the purpose of the group obscure, Clarke was offered command, but he refused, preferring to return to his desert roots in Cairo. For the first few months, the war office found it difficult to find a new head for such an innovative and off-kilter department.

The appointment of Colonel John Bevan on June 1st, 1942 provided the LCS with much needed stability, and he recruited Ronald Wingate, who had served with the Ministry of Economic Warfare. The three men, including Dennis Wheatley, had both the experience and imagination to bring the LCS into a more major role in the War Office's main planning of the war.

With John Bevan as director in London, Dudley Clarke in the Middle East, and Peter Fleming (previously of Auxiliary Units and SOE) taking control of Far East deceptions, the personnel became permanent.

Journalist and espionage historian, Anthony Cave Brown, later wrote that the London Controlling Section was Churchill's "greatest single contribution to military theory and practice."

The build-up of American forces in Britain, with the purpose of invading Europe, brought a new problem. In April 1943, since the LCS answered directly to Churchill's War Office, John Bevan encouraged a new department to be formed, answerable directly to the whole of Allied Command (Eisenhower and the US command). The new unit, Ops (B), was commanded by General Frederick Morgan.

ID card of fictitious Captain William Martin, the "Man Who Never was"

## Operation Mincemeat

In the early months of 1943, Dennis Wheatley and Ian Fleming both claimed a role in of one of the most ingenious disinformation operations of the war.

To disguise an Allied attack on Sicily in 1943, fictional plans about a coming invasion of Sardinia and Greece were planted on a corpse dressed as a Royal Marines major. The body was dropped by a British submarine near a Spanish shore, leading the Nazis to believe they had found Britain's secret war objective. "I was one of the half-dozen officers who planned Operation Mincemeat," Wheatley wrote later to a friend.

The Famous Photo of Jean Leslie, a friend of one of LCS's secretary's, placed in Captain William Martin's wallet

The body was duly washed ashore in Spain, examined by German agents, and the documents copied. The German High Command fell for it hook, line and sinker. The Nazis diverted air power, and Greece was strengthened by three panzer divisions.

The landings in Sicily were lightly defended, and allied losses were minimal.

Incidentally, an upshot of LCS was the American innovation of 'Beach Jumpers'. Douglas Fairbanks Jnr, Hollywood actor, after being attached to Mountbatten, was responsible for deception in the role of 'beach Jumpers', who attacked beaches far away from the main landings in Sicily, and broadcast widely, diverting resources from the main battlefield.

Since all the departments knew each other, and coordinated some deceptions together, it is difficult to give any single credit to any agency for any specific operation. With this in mind, I credit 'A' Force, the LCS and Ops (B) equally.

Here's a list of some of the other deceptions planned by the joint deception departments, hopefully in some form of chronological order...

**Operation Cascade**; A successful deception in 1942, to create a false presence of Allied troops in the Mediterranean theatre, using bogus troop formations, radio traffic and double agents.

**Operation Bertram**; A deception by Montgomery, Sept 1942, at the second battle of El-Alamein. Using blow up tanks and wooden guns, Rommel was deceived to commit forces elsewhere.

**Operation Cockade**; A series of deceptions in late 1943 to confuse the Germans of proposed allied landings. The operation was not a success, but did help the success of subsequent similar plans.

**Operation Cockade**; Deception operations in late 1943 to alleviate both German pressure on Allied operations in Sicily and on the Soviets on the Eastern Front, by feinting attacks into Western Europe.

**Operation Copperhead**; A deception in 1944 using a double for Field Marshal Montgomery (M. E. Clifton James), to deceive the Germans into thinking D-day would fall in the Mediterranean.

**Operation Ferdinand**; A deception to place Genoa, Italy as the site for D-day, and kept German troops in the area until July 1944.

**Operation Accumulator**; A deception after D-day to suggest a second landing would be in the Pas-de-Calais. This kept German divisions near Calais while the Allies established a beachhead in Normandy.

**Operation Barclay**; A deception tasking the Balkans as the next Allied target, not Sicily. Hitler believed it. Used in concert with Operation Mincemeat, the Germans reduced the armies in Sicily. Greece was strengthened by three panzer divisions.

**Operation Boardman**; A deception that continued the false threat of an Allied invasion of the Balkans.

**Operation Chettyford**; A deception in support of the 1944 Allied invasion at Anzio, to misinform the Germans that a major invasion of the Balkans was planned.

In February, 1944, London Control, a shorter name the men inside the unit were using, began their biggest deception of the war. It would change history, and shorten the war by many years.

**Operation Bodyguard** was named after Churchill's famous speech to Stalin: "In wartime, truth is so precious that she should always be attended by a bodyguard of lies", and was actually a combination of 36 separate small operations.

Hitler knew the allies were going to invade France, they just didn't know exactly where. London Control's job was to confuse the Germans to such a degree, that they believed the obfuscation, not the plan itself.

To assist their plans of deception, the allies had four very distinct advantages.

General George Patton; royally upset he did not lead Allied forces on D-day

One; they had already successfully deceived the Germans on the landings in North Africa, Operation Torch had been a resounding victory in the LCS's history.

Two; the RAF had total control of the skies over England, making air reconnaissance very difficult for the Luftwaffe

Three; they actually had control over every single Nazi spy in Britain; every single one had become a double agent.

Four; they had broken the enigma code years before, and now had absolute proof that their lies were turning German heads. They had specific communications which mentioned their deceptions; the Nazis were swallowing the whole of Operation Bodyguard.

LCS set to work; they threatened Norway, yet again, forcing Hitler to reinforce an already over-heavy concentration of troops. They confused the position of British and allied commanders. They inflated the actual number of divisions in Britain from 52 to over 80.

A million imaginary men were stationed in East Anglia, north of London; the 'United States First Army Group', led by the famous General Patton himself.

Backed up by bogus radio traffic, phone calls, and dummy trucks, tanks and landing craft, the news of this group reached Hitler himself. Because of the deception of these inflated numbers, the German High Command believed the 'raid' on Normandy was just a feint to draw Rommel away from the channel; Patton was going to land in the Pas de Calais a week later.

To Hitler and his Chiefs of Staff, an invasion of France without Patton was simply unthinkable; how could the allies leave their best commander behind?

Operation Bodyguard was a total success, achieving complete tactical surprise.

On the 6th June, 1944, the first waves of paratroopers landed in Normandy with hardly a shot being fired against them. 160,000 troops sailed a hundred miles in complete safety. A whole floating Mulberry dock system was transported from England to Normandy. Supported by hundreds of naval craft, thousands of amphibious landing craft hit the French beachheads bringing troops, tanks, trucks, and men.

Rommel was at home for his wife's birthday.

German High Command didn't wake Hitler until ten o'clock, believing the news of Normandy landings insufficiently important to wake the Führer. Hitler woke ten hours after the airborne infiltration had begun, and three and a half hours after the actual assault on the beaches.

Now, the beaches were defended, and yes, allied soldiers faced deadly opposition, especially on Omaha Beach, which was defended by one of the Germans' best divisions in northwestern France. But no troops had been sent to reinforce them for a sustained assault. The invasion of June 6th was a complete surprise.

Even as the allies poured men and equipment onshore, vulnerable in both their numbers and their strategic position, Hitler held steadfast to his belief that Normandy was a feint. By mid-July, the Allies had brought 30 divisions ashore in Normandy, but there were still 22 German divisions sitting in Pas de Calais, waiting for General Patton and the "real" invasion. Hitler did not begin to release them until July 27.

It was too late.

The British use of the new science of strategic deception has no precedent in military history; Wingate, the historian, called it "almost a new weapon." The offices of deception had almost single-handedly won the war; London Controlling Section and Ops (B) had ensured that only one side turned up for the biggest battle of the war.

# The Military Intelligence Dept 9 (MI9)

Originally given the unwieldy title of "British Directorate of Military Intelligence Section 9", MI9 officially came into being on 23 December 1939, by Major Norman Crockatt, formerly of The Royal Scots.

However its inclusion in 'Churchill's Secret Armies' sees MI9's real beginnings as December 1941, when it broke away from its vastly bigger family and struck out on its own.

Originally formed to assist the return of downed RAF air crew, its purview soon outgrew the constructs of its originators. At first MI9 was located in Room 424 of the Metropole Hotel, Northumberland Avenue, London, but after becoming its own entity, the department moved to Wilton Park, Buckinghamshire.

**For PoW's; German money was hidden inside gramophone records**

**Pre-Flight Training** was used to teach the pilots and air crew of the basics in avoiding capture, and the probable sources of friendly faces in the black country behind-enemy-lines.

**Clandestine Devices** and aids were given to the air crew, described later.

**Networks of Resistance Groups** were set up (usually with SOE planning and execution) to bring Air crew home. This was not an easy task, and dangers were faced by both air-crews and native civilians. These groups were serviced by SOE drops or units such as Operation Carpetbagger, and air crew were retrieved by boat, submarine or by Lysander aircraft.

### Prisoner Of War Liaison
MI9 communicated with British prisoners of war and sent them advice and equipment.

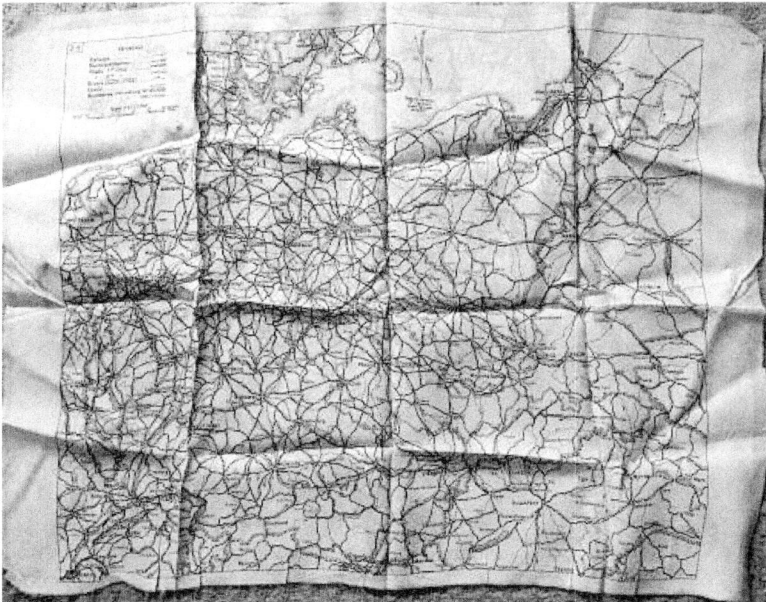

Detailed European maps printed on thin silk cloth, saved many lives

### CHRISTOPHER HUTTON
A whole department was set up under a McGuyver type character called Christopher Hutton. He invented both per-capture (to aid the user evade capture) and post-capture (to aid the user after capture, ie; for PoW's to escape again) aids.

**Hutton Printed Maps**; accurate maps printed onto silk using fast inks by John Bartholomew, a top class printer who gave his designs free. When used as handkerchiefs or sewn into underwear, were invaluable to the escaping airmen. Over 400,000 silk maps of Europe were printed.

**Hutton Compasses** were made by Blunt Brothers, so small, they could be secreted in the back of a button. All aircrew uniforms contained one screwable button with a compass inside. When prison guards got wise to the reversed threads which just tightened the screws, Hutton magnetized razor blades on which the G of 'Gillette' always pointed north when dangled by a thread.

Maps, ID cards, and official travel documents were hidden inside playing cards

**Uniforms and Clothing**; blankets were sent to PoW's with clothes patterns drawn in invisible ink. These lines would become visible when soaked in water, enabling future escapees to make civilian-style clothing.

**Hutton Flying Boots** were designed with hollow heels to hide maps and escape equipment, and easily modified to look like civilian shoes.

**Hutton Escape Kits** were in a small cigarette tin designed to carry a small supply of powdered food and foreign currency, razor blades, water-purifying tablets and a rubber water bottle. By 1941, all British aircrew carried these.

Hutton 'Escape Knife: this multi-tool included a strong blade, a screwdriver, three saws, a lock pick, and a wire cutter.

Jasper Maskelyne, a practicing magician, designed hiding places for escape aids; objects hidden in cricket bats and baseball bats, maps disguised as playing cards and actual money in board-games.

Waddingtons supplied 'special' editions of Monopoly board games. Monopoly, snakes and ladders, chess sets and playing cards contained concealed maps, compasses, real money, forged German identity cards, ration coupons and forged travel warrants.

It is estimated that up to 35,000 British and other Allied troops who managed to escape and make their way back to Allied territory did so with Hutton's and MI9's maps and equipment.

# CHURCHILL'S SECRET ARMIES

# THE ORIGINS OF OPERATION PLUTO

Floating drum to be wound by 80 miles of pipeline & laid in a single night

Looking forward two years to the landings on D-day, Churchill foresaw the problems of fuel supply to a conquering and advancing army. Without huge supplies of fuels of many types, the invasion would grind to a halt, and any pause in gaining a foothold would give Germany time to re-group and counter-attack.

Churchill determined quickly that taking such fuel supplies across by ship would entail terrible losses both to U-Boats and the Luftwaffe; another safer, more permanent solution had to be found.

After various trials it was decided to manufacture flexible steel pipelines to deliver the fuel, and that a length of 80 miles would be the required initial length of each pipeline.

The tar covered steel pipeline was welded together from 30 foot sections, then into sections of ¼ mile, then welded to 80 miles at it was rolled onto large hollow drums (each 1600 tons in weight) installed on board specially converted ships.

However, even laying a pipeline across the channel (a 70 mile distance from England to Normandy) had to be done in one single night to avoid U-Boat attention. The large drums holding 80 miles of pipe were rolled on the sea's surface, dropping the pipeline into the sea in one operation, giving fuel to the D-day beaches by August, 1944, delivered from the Isle of Wight to Cherbourg.

From Normandy, the allies extended the pipelines as they advanced across Europe, across France, Belgium and Germany. In all over 1000 miles of pipeline were laid.

By the end of the war, over 1,000,000 gallons of fuel (gasoline, petrol, diesel and oil) were being pumped to Europe every single day.

At each end of the pipeline, the feed was brought ashore, and distributed to many fixed outlets

At the end of the war, the British Government managed to salvage over 90% of the pipe, selling it for far more than the cost of the salvage.

# ROYAL AIR FORCE COMMANDOS

Foreseeing the need for a technical-based fighting force as the army advanced eastward across Africa, and headed towards Europe, the RAF formed their own commando units in 1942.

At the height of the allied advances, fifteen such units were available, each 150 strong. These specifically-trained units contained technicians, ground crew, and armorers. They were used in North Africa, Sicily, Italy, and Europe.

RAF Commandoes in Italy, stripping parts from a Spitfire

Their main job was the capture of enemy airfields in an intact condition, and they were used in conjunction with other special forces to great effect.

Not only were allied fighters able to utilize the new front-line airfields, but the RAF Commandoes captured intact enemy fighters, servicing them and using them against the Nazis.

As the allies swept across Germany, some experimental aircraft were captured.

The RAF Commandoes captured some intact Nazi experimental aircraft

# THE SPECIAL DUTIES SQUADRONS

Several squadrons of the RAF were seconded to the intelligence departments during the war, each operating in far stricter secrecy than normal RAF units.

No 357 Special Duties Squadron; note the SOE adaption of fixed steps

**No. 138 (Special Duties) Squadron**, was formed in August, 1941, to perform missions in occupied France, Holland and Belgium for the Special Operations Executive (SOE). Its primary task was to assist SOE to maintain clandestine contact with the French Resistance

The SOE adapted their Lysanders' rear cockpit to allow room for two very uncomfortable, crammed passengers, the Lysander could insert and remove agents from the continent or retrieve Allied aircrew shot down over occupied territory. To hasten access to the rear cockpit, and cut down vulnerable time on the ground, the Mk IIIs were fitted with a fixed ladder over the left-hand side. The Lysander missions were almost completely made under cover of darkness, and the aircraft were painted matt black.

The Lysanders of 138 Squadron flew from secret airfields near Newmarket and Tempsford, although they did land at regular RAF stations to re-fuel before crossing the channel, particularly at RAF Tangmere. Flying by the light of the moon and without any navigation equipment other than a map and compass, Lysanders would land on short strips of land marked out by four or five torches.

**No. 161 (Special Duties) Squadron** was also a highly secretive unit of the Royal Air Force, tasked with similar missions for the Special Operations Executive.

No 161 Special Duties Squadron, tasked to Special Operations Executive (SOE)

**No. 1586 (Polish Special Duties) Flight** was formed on 4th November 1943 from the remnants of 301 (Polish) Squadron and equipped with Handley Page Halifax II medium bombers. 1586 Flight performed partisan supply drops and agent insertion.

No 138 Special Duties Squadron, 1943, (Polish Section) based at Tempsford

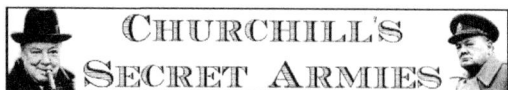

# THE INTELLIGENCE SERVICES IN THE PACIFIC

To save writing a dozen short chapters on the various intelligence networks of the South Pacific, I have attempted to list them all together here. I only hope that to the reader, it all still makes a modicum of sense.

At the outbreak of war in the Western Pacific, only two intelligence services were operational in the area, Secret Intelligence Australia (SIA), and the Coastwatchers networks.

### Secret Intelligence Australia (SIA)

Secret Intelligence Australia (SIA) was a British intelligence unit working out of London, reporting directly to MI6, and thus also directly to the SOE. It eventually became Section B of the Allied Intelligence Bureau, but was always an independent unit, not accountable to the Australians or the Americans. The information gathered by the SIA came to London first, then was distributed back to the AIB.

A great deal of information gathered came from Muslim civilians and native religious leaders, who considered the Japanese as a threat to Islamic solidarity. The Japanese began a propaganda war, which the SIA answered in kind.

Agents trained at Caboolture, Queensland and the Z Experimental Station in Cairns.

### The Coastwatchers

The Coastwatchers were a series of groups of military intelligence operatives stationed on remote Pacific islands. They observed enemy movements, and signaled their local headquarters either with radio or searchlight. News was then transmitted to whatever intelligence agencies paid the most.

Britain (SIA), Australia, New Zealand, and the Netherlands all had some form of Coastwatcher networks.

Coastwatchers on Guadalcanal gave the allies crucial information before the initial assault began. It is thought their information saved hundreds of lives.

Coastwatchers in Guadalcanal provided essential intelligence for the allies

### The General Picture

After the bombing of Pearl Harbor, the two biggest Allies in the area, United States of America and Australia, immediately had differing problems on their hands.

In the first months of 1942, not driven by Hitler's rise and the war in Europe, the USA simply had not needed an intelligence agency of its own. Now they had to fight a rearguard action across a thousand islands, 4000 miles from their homeland.

Intelligence was to play a major part. However, at the time, the USA had no military intelligence service to speak of.

Wild Bill Donovan's office of the Coordinator of Information (COI), had certainly set the ball rolling but he had recruited socialites, hardly the stuff for jungle operations. The COI had morphed quickly into the Office of Strategic Services (OSS), but as yet was still in a very fledgling stage, copiously copying everything the SOE had done.

Agents were quickly trained, in Canada and in the new camps set up in the USA.

Australian forces, New Guinea, 1944. Note the adapted Sten machine guns

Australian forces had been involved in the European war since its beginnings, but relied on British Intelligence information. After Pearl Harbor, the Second World War had literally arrived on Australia's doorstep. Singapore had fallen in February 1942, and after advancing through Burma and Sumatra, the Australians were certain that their homeland was next. With communications from Britain considered 'scetchy' at best, there was a sudden necessity for the countries directly involved against the Japanese to have their own military intelligence gathering agencies.

There are conflicting stories about how the ball got rolling, but suffice to say, that when it did, it was instantly authorized and recognized by every player in the game. To continue the football analogy, it made sense for the Australians to be the first to kick the ball.

### Inter-Allied Services Department (IASD)

Formed in March 1942, it was initially called the Inter-Allied Services Department (IASD), and was modelled directly on the British Special Operations Executive (SOE) in London (hence the inclusion in the book). With offices in Melbourne British SOE Officers recently escaped from Singapore becoming the nucleus of the growing operation, in more familiar terms it was soon renamed Special Operations Australia

(SOA). In 1943 the SOA became known as the Services Reconnaissance Department (SRD), and for once the name stuck.

Now officially linked to the Allied Intelligence Bureau, SRD oversaw all intelligence-gathering, reconnaissance and raiding missions in Japanese-occupied areas of New Guinea, the Dutch East Indies (Indonesia), Portuguese Timor (East Timor), the Malayan Peninsula, British Borneo and Singapore.

Australians from the 2/3 Independent Companies in New Guinea, July, 1943

Again, modelling itself on the highly successful SOE models, new training schools were established in various locations all across Australia;

Camp Z in Refuge Bay north of Sydney
Z Experimental Station ("House on the Hill" or ZES.) near Cairns, Queensland
Fraser Commando School on Fraser Island, Queensland
Careening Bay Camp, (Special Boat Section) on Garden Island, Western Australia
Caboolture Training Camp, Queensland

## Allied Intelligence Bureau (AIB)

Formed in June 1942, the AIB was a joint allied venture, incorporating the information centers of no less than ten different intelligence networks.

In time United States, Australian, Dutch and British intelligence agencies learned to work together, to share information, to share men and equipment scattered throughout the area, to coordinate the distribution of propaganda, and to coordinate parties of spies, commandos, native contingents and special forces working behind Japanese lines.

Because of the Allied Intelligence Bureau, the collection of intelligence and the guerrilla warfare waged against Japanese forces in the South West Pacific was organized on a far larger scale than the Japanese realized, any success were duplicated, and lessons learned by all sections from failures.

The AIB was divided into four sections;

'A' Section; focused on information collection and commando operations.

'B' Section; basically Secret Intelligence Australia (SIA) focused on general intelligence.

'C' Section; gathered field intelligence from Coastwatchers, natives and civilians.

'D' Section; Far Eastern Liaison Office which organized anti-Japanese propaganda.

## The Main Agencies at the Center of it All

Ten different intelligence agencies worked together...

Donovan's newly formed American Office of Strategic Services (OSS)

The Australian Services Reconnaissance Department (SRD), formerly SOA

Secret Intelligence Australia (SIA)

The Netherlands East Indies Forces Intelligence Service (NEIFIS)

Netherlands Indies Government Information Service (NIGIS)

Men of Z Special Unit, the operational side of the intelligence services

Various Special Forces groups were formed for operational use, mainly Z Special Unit.

## THE 712TH SURVEY FLOTILLA

In October 1943, the 712th Survey Flotilla was created with probably the most dangerous and secret missions of the war. It is also the final 'Secret Army' that I discovered, thus making it in my case, the most secret of *Churchill's Secret Armies*.

(I list it here because of its importance to the next chapter, the Mulberry Harbors.)

After the disaster of the raid on Dieppe, the importance of finding the best part of the French coast for the site of the Allied landings on D-Day took far greater significance.

The area needed three distinct criteria;

It had to be relatively close to the British coast.

It had to have a flat disposition to land numbers of troops and men.

It had to be lightly defended.

It had to have the 'right' type of sand on the beach that would allow armored vehicles to transfer quickly.

It had to have a shallow enough beach for landing craft, yet have a deep basin close to the shore for the building of temporary harbors for the disembarking of equipment from larger ships.

**Shallow draft Landing Craft; these boats were perfect for beach surveys**

## Combined Operations Pilotage Parties

Their job was the surveying of landing sites for invasions, including those of Sicily and Normandy. These parties were made up of members of the Royal Navy, Royal Marines, Corps of Royal Engineers and Special Boat Service (SBS). This included the 712th Survey Flotilla, in Hamble.

The 712th Survey Flotilla was a small cadre of hydrographers (scientists who study the sea bed, sea currents, depth, etc) brought together and tasked with the secret survey of possible D-Day landing sites. Based at HMS Tormentor, a Royal Navy landing craft base, between Southampton and Portsmouth on the south coast of England, they undertook missions along the French coast.

They used a landing craft for these missions, and took extensive, detailed depth readings, and physical samples of the sea floor. They also landed on beaches, testing the solidity of the sand on the beach and took samples. It was crucial that the sand on the beaches chosen for D-Day would take the punishment of thousands of vehicles, and not get bogged down.

Between November 1943 and January 1944, the 712th Survey Flotilla undertook many missions to the French coast.

Operation KJF, one of many, took place on the night of 26[th]November; three landing craft took measurements off the French port of Arromanches, near the future 'Gold Beach', and the location for Mulberry B.

The final survey, Operation Bellpush Charlie, took place on the night of 30th January 30, 1944, just four months from D-day.

These scientist surveyors were unsung heroes, and risked their lives for the information they gathered.

# THE MULBERRY HARBOR

Unbelievably, the earliest idea for the use of temporary harbors to aid a beachhead was sketched in 1917 by Winston Churchill in a World War 1 memo to then Prime Minister, Lloyd George.

Three months before the failure of the raid on Dieppe in August 1942, Winston Churchill issued a memo 'Piers for use on beaches', seeking a solution to the problem of establishing a deep-water harbor at an invasion point. All concerned with the project knew that there was little point in attacking an already existing harbor town and too much of a bottle-neck to break out of. The problem was simple; a deep water harbor would have to be created.

"They must float up and down with the tide," Churchill said. "The anchor problem must be mastered. Let me have the best solution worked out. Don't argue the matter. The difficulties will argue for themselves."

The only problems were; how to build them, how to get them to the landing site, and how to get vehicles and equipment from the Concrete parts in deep water to the beaches. It became apparent that the one project had three distinct and very different parts.

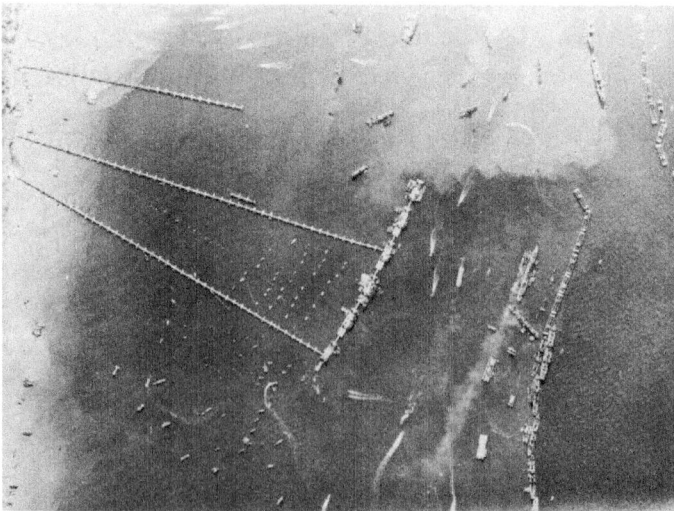

Mulberry B near Gold Beach, Oct 27th, 1944, showing calmer water inshore

### The Breakwater

For ships to sail accurately to the floating wharf and not damage it or crash into it, they needed calm sea conditions, so it was decided to build a breakwater on the sea side, a barrier to the Atlantic, providing calmer water inshore.

### The Deep Water Harbor

There needed to be a harbor wharf, a structure set on the sea floor yet rising and falling with the tide to allow ships to sail alongside, unload their vehicles, men and equipment, and sail off.

### The Roadway

There needed to be a roadway from the deep water of the concrete harbor, across the bay, to the beach itself. This roadway must be able to deal with both the rise and fall of the tide, and the occasional storm.


### MULBERRY CAISSONS

The final concrete Mulberry, or Caisson, seems to have been a result of a combination of designers; I cannot find one inventor named responsible. They were such an extensive undertaking; they were built at over 15 different shipbuilders around Britain. Each part weighed between 2,000 and 6,000 tons, were floated, towed by 2 tug boats and gathered together along the southern coast of England. These were then sunk, waiting to be re-floated for transport to France, hence the common 'Phoenix' name.


### The Floating Wharf and Bridges

Three separate designs were brought to the prototype stage, and a trial was set up at Cairn Head, Galloway, on the Solway Firth. Over a few weeks, they were subjected to severe weather.

Civil Engineer, Hugh Hughes developed what he called his "Hippo" piers and "Crocodile" bridge spans.

Ronald Hamilton described his invention as the "Swiss Roll" which consisted of a floating canvas roadway, waterproofed and stiffened with slats. The whole apparatus was held together by tensioned cables.

Major Allan Beckett (War Office's 'Transportation 5 Department' (Tn5)) had designed a floating bridge tied to the sea floor with what he called 'kite anchors'. This was linked to a floating pier head which raised and lowered with the tide on fixed anchored legs.

After the storms, thanks in great part to his kite anchors, Beckett's design was the only one left standing.

Perfect for getting men ashore and the safe and quick removal of casualties

## Gooseberries, Bombardons, Whales, Beatles, Spuds and Corncobs

The artificial harbors needed sheltered waters (in order to be positioned properly and accurately, for ships to sail, anchor, and discharge their cargo). It was decided to take old ships, called Corncobs, which would be sunk, causing a breakwater from the Atlantic swell. On D-Day over 80 ships were sailed across and sunk in place on all five assault beaches. This would give smoother sea conditions (Gooseberries) for the positioning of the Caissons and harbor construction.

In addition to the Corncobs, the Navy used floating 'x' shaped devices, anchored to the sea floor to further calm the waves.

(This next sentence is comedic, but it must be remembered, code words were used continually to confuse German spies)

The Phoenixes would be towed into the Gooseberries and placed behind the Corncobs and Bombardons.

It gets worse...

The bridge parts of Beckett's design (that vehicles drove on) were called 'whales'.

The floating pontoon parts (on which each end of the 80ft whales sat) were called 'beatles'.

And the floating pier heads inshore of the Caissons were called 'spuds'.

**Sherman tanks drive off ships, directly onto the beachhead, note the whales and beetles**

On the afternoon of the 6th June, 1944, (Operation Overlord +1) with the soldiers already fighting on the beaches, a fleet of 1000 Corncob ships and Caisson tugboats sailed 60 miles across the English channel, towing over 400 different parts to the five Allied beaches.

Considering the confusion already in the area, it is a wonder of modern engineering and planning.

Corncobs were sunk at every beach, providing calmer waters for naval craft and the transfer of soldiers and wounded.

Larger full-size ports were planned for Gold and Omaha.

As early as D-Day+2, June 9th, the construction of 2 full Mulberry harbors, one at Omaha Beach and one at Gold Beach were initiated. Allan Beckett was on hand at Arrowmanches, near Gold beach to supervise the installation there. The Mulberry at Arrowmanches was soon christened 'Port Winston'. By the 18th, both harbors were working.

Soon piers bristled with anti-aircraft guns, and large barrage balloons to discourage enemy aircraft from making low bombing runs.

Damage to Omaha Mulberry after the storm of June 21st, 1944

It should be noted here that neither the British Navy nor the American Engineers had much confidence in Beckett's claims on the safety and security of his newly designed "kite anchors', and did not use them extensively on their installations. The Caissons at Omaha beach were not attached by them, nor were the Bombardons at Gold Beach.

### Storm of June 21st
A storm raged for three days from the 19th June, damaging Omaha Mulberry extensively, although the Americans adapted their unloading style to suit. The Bombardons at Gold Beach (the Navy's responsibility, and therefore not held with Beckett's kite anchors) were also damaged. The whole of Beckett's roadway system at Gold beach, supervised by him, and fastened with his kite anchors, was not damaged.

Although the storm damaged the Mulberrys, the figures of these artificial harbors are staggering.

Port Winston, although only designed for three months use, was used for over eight months. Two and a half million men were landed, and over half a million vehicles.

Over ten miles of floating roadway were transported and used at the beaches.

When no longer in use, most of the 'whales' were taken away and placed across rivers in France to replace bridges damaged in the war.

Some of the concrete Caissons are still visible and visited today, in France and around Britain, after seventy years.

# THE 30 ASSAULT UNIT

Formed in Sept 1942, 30 Assault Unit was initially called 30 Advanced Unit, or 30 Commando. It was possibly inspired by the German Abwehrkommando, a unit headed by Otto Skorzeny, who advanced with forward forces, or sometimes ahead of them, grabbing personnel, intelligence, codes, documents, or equipment before it could be destroyed or recalled.

**30 Assault Unit, June 1944, accept the surrender of German HQ personnel**

A brainchild of Lord Louis Mountbatten and Ian Fleming, the unit was drawn from all four arms of the British Military, and trained in unarmed combat, safe-cracking and lock-picking at many of the SOE facilities.

Its first action was during the failed Raid on Dieppe. 50 members of 30 Assault Unit landed in Dieppe with the sole purpose of getting to the town's police headquarters and stealing the new four-rotor enigma machine. Neither the main force nor 30 Assault Unit reached the main streets, never mind the Police HQ. There is some thought that suggest the raid had been cancelled, then reinstated just to get the enigma machine, but this is not corroborated in any way.

The unit was also involved in Operation torch, and landed as a diversion to the west of Algiers at Sidi Ferruch on 8 November. Provided with detailed maps and photographs of the area they located the Italian naval headquarters, and captured battle orders for the German and Italian fleets, current code books and other documents.

The unit served in Greece, Norway, Sicily, Italy, and Corsica.

In June 1944, now officially called 30 Assault Unit, they landed on Juno beach and Utah beach, tasked to capture a radar station at Douvres-la-Delivrande which did not surrender until 17 June. They later fought their way into Cherbourg, and followed the Free French forces into Paris, and in mounted a series of armed Jeep raids (Operation Crossbow), captured V-1 sites along the Channel coast ports.

30 Assault Unit, with a captured German flag, probably May, 1945

Near the end of the war, in May 1945, 30 Assault Unit captured the German Naval Base in Bremen.

After 1943, Fleming had less and less control of the unit, calling them his 'Red Indians', a name the men hated. He would use the phrase 5 times in his first book, Casino Royale.

In 2011, 30 Assault Unit was the subject of a motion picture, starring Sean Bean, called *'Age of Heroes'*.

# THE ROYAL NAVAL COMMANDOS

In the early amphibious landings of the war, the objective of getting men ashore was hampered by poor organization of the beachhead itself. To help alleviate the problem, the Royal Navy formed a new unit, the Royal Naval Beach Parties. Their task would be to direct the flow of landing craft, the quick facilitation of men ashore, and the subsequent removal of the landing craft.

Royal Naval commandoes, in charge of the beach, D-day, June 1944

**Operation Ironclad;** in the landings against Vichy French in Madagascar, the Royal Naval Beach Parties landed with Commandoes on the beaches. Their job was to direct the Commandoes and to take control of the beachhead.

Due to the smooth flow of troops onto their objective, the mission was a total success, and it was quickly decided to form permanent units, each trained in Scotland at the Commando Training Schools.

In late 1942, the Royal Naval Commandos were raised. By the end of the war, 22 companies existed to establish, maintain and control beachheads during amphibious operations. They worked in every theatre, and performed in every amphibious operation until the end of the war (including Operation Torch, D-Day, and crossing the Rhine in Operation Market Garden).

They were disbanded at the end of the war.

# THE HOBART FUNNIES

Despite their odd name, these innovative tank adaptions saved lives on D-Day and other amphibious landings.

In the 1942 raid on Dieppe, the lack of mobility from the landing craft to the shore resulted in many vehicles getting bogged down in the pebble beach.

The war Office (and therefore Churchill) knew this problem had to be conquered before a full-scale allied landing on mainland Europe could be attempted.

A Churchill tank climbs over a 'Hobart 33', to scale a sea wall

The job was given to Major General Percy Hobart, a career soldier, and the father-in-law of Field Marshall Bernard (Monty) Montgomery.

Hobart had transferred to the Royal Tank Corps in 1923, and had been involved in armored warfare ever since. Although technically too old for service (he was 57, and had to be personally reinstated by Churchill after being 'retired' in 1940) he set to his task, both utilizing existing designs and concepts, and inventing new ones.

Called 'Hobart's Funnies' because of their peculiar and unusual amendment to regular design, they saved lives in every subsequent amphibious landing. The vehicles were used extensively on D-day, but only by British and Canadian troops. The Americans did not like the ideas, and used only one variant (the Sherman). They have subsequently been criticized for this inaction, and it is commonly believed that lives could have been saved on American beachheads if the Commanders had used Hobart's devices.

Some examples...

**ARC (Armoured Ramp Carrier):** a Churchill tank without a turret with extendable ramps at either end; vehicles would drive up the ramps and over the tank body to cross obstacles.

The Hobart 'Flying Dustbin', capable of firing a 40lb 'bomb', 150 yards

**AVRE (Armoured Vehicle Royal Engineers):** A Churchill tank's main gun replaced by a Petard Mortar that fired a forty-pound (18 kg) HE-filled projectile (nicknamed the "Flying dustbin") range 150 yards.

**BARV (BEACH ARMOURED RECOVERY VEHICLE):** a waterproofed Sherman tank (able to operate in water 9 feet deep), to remove vehicles that had become broken-down or swamped in the surf and were blocking access to the beaches.

A Hobart 'Bobbin'; to enable heavy vehicles to traverse beaches

**BOBBIN**: a Churchill tank with a reel of 10-foot (3.0 m) wide canvas cloth carried in front, to unroll onto the ground to form a "path" on soft ground.

**BULLSHORN PLOUGH:** a Churchill tank with a mine plough in front to expose and make harmless any land mines.

**CANAL DEFENCE LIGHT**: A powerful carbon-arc searchlight carried on several types of tank inside a modified turret.

Centaur Bulldozer, a completely armored earth-mover, used on D-Day

**CENTAUR BULLDOZER**: a Cromwell tank with the turret removed and fitted with a simple winch-operated bulldozer blade.

A Hobart Crab, on a Sherman, one of the few variations the US troops used

**CRAB**: A Sherman tank with a mine flail at the front, a rotating cylinder of weighted chains to explode mines in the path of the tank.

**CROCODILE**: a Churchill tank with a flame-thrower in place of the hull machine gun, with a range of 120 yards. An armored trailer, towed behind the tank, carried 400 Imperial gallons of fuel.

An amphibious Sherman, fitted with Hobart's waterproof canvas adaption

**DD TANK:** an amphibious Sherman tank fitted with a watertight canvas housing able to float and reach the shore after launching from a landing craft.

A Hobart 'Double Onion'; demolition charges to blow a gun emplacement or wall

**DOUBLE ONION:** a Churchill tank with two large demolition charges on a metal frame that could be placed against a concrete wall and detonated from a safe distance.

Basically, the Fascine was a ditch filler.

**FASCINE**: a Churchill tank with a bundle of wooden poles or brushwood lashed together with wires carried in front of the tank that could be released to fill a ditch.

Called a 'Small Box Girder, this could span a 30 feet span and be deployed in 30 seconds

**SMALL BOX GIRDER**: a Churchill tank with an assault bridge carried in front to be dropped to span a 30-foot gap in 30 seconds.

# THE OPERATION JEDBURGH

Operation Jedburgh was a combined SOE/OSS/BCRA operation to encourage resistance behind enemy lines during and after D-Day. It was named after the Scottish town, and in particular the scots raiders who came down from the hills, stole English livestock, and vanished north without a trace. There is a steep blunt-ended valley near Jedburgh called the *Devil's Beeftub*, named after the raids where the Scots led their stolen cattle and sheep.

Jedburgh Team; 'Ian'. I had to include the team with my own name

Operation Jedburgh was the first time these three organisations had ever worked so closely together; a cooperation of the SOE, and the two organisations it had itself spawned, the American OSS, and the Free French BCRA.

Broken down into three man teams, each team consisted of; one person in charge, a second person, and a radio operator. Where possible, the teams would include one Briton, one American, and one native of the country to be infiltrated.

In all, 83 American, 90 British, 103 French, 5 Belgian, and 5 Dutch personnel were extensively trained in paramilitary techniques for Jedburgh missions. Ninety-three Jedburgh teams parachuted into France and eight went into The Netherlands.

Never intended or trained to be a long-term operation, these Jedburgh units were used from D-day on June 6th, to Operation Market Garden.

**Jedburgh Team; 'Frederick', dropped into northern France on 9th June, 1944**

In 1944 the SOE did not have the airpower to perform such a huge task on their own, their aircraft were in constant use, and they had none to spare. The Jedburgh teams were dropped by the USAF from B-24 Liberators, usually used in Operation Carperbagger; an ongoing supply of equipment and ammunition for the resistance in Europe.

The mission of each unit was painstakingly researched. Some parachuted in with explosives to do one job, others arrived with containers of hundreds of machine guns and ammunition. Some had a solo task, others were to create a concentrated war zone.

Jedburgh Team; 'Ronald'. They were dropped into France on 4th Aug 1944

### Operation Jedburgh

The teams were trained thoroughly in SOE training schools, then transported to RAF bases for insertion.

On the days approaching 6th June, the Jedburgh teams were dropped by parachute into Nazi-occupied France, the Netherlands and Belgium. Some teams' aims were to conduct acts of sabotage and guerrilla warfare, most to lead the local resistance forces or Maquis groups in group or mass actions against the Germans. Their main function was to provide a personal communication link between the guerrillas and the Allied command in Britain. Agents on the ground could provide liaison with command, advice on tactics, technical expertise and experienced leadership, but their most powerful asset was their ability to arrange airdrops of arms and ammunition.

Normal SOE parachute drops delivered the operative in civilian clothes, armed with only a spade to bury the parachute and a pistol or Sten machine gun. The Jedburgh agents, however, were allowed to travel in full combat uniform, with M1 carbine and Colt Automatic pistol. In addition to their sabotage equipment, the teams dropped with the Type B Mark II radio, more commonly referred to as the B2 or "Jed Set", critical for communicating with Special Force Headquarters in London. Pieces of silk with likely radio phrases were replaced with a series of four letter codes to save the time spent in transmitting.

They carried full ration packs, medical supplies, binoculars and maps. These men were not dropped to perform long covert missions, but to gather forces and immediately rise in open attacks.

The Jedburgh teams were a great success, with few casualties. After their achievements in Europe, they were used in the Far East for the short period before VJ-Day.

The damage caused by both the Jedburgh teams and the French resistance is difficult to collate, but on the night before D-Day it is estimated that in the Normandy area over 50 locomotives were destroyed, and the railway lines were cut in 500 places.

It is partly due to these units that the D-day beaches were cut off from swift retaliation by Axis forces.

# THE AUTHOR'S AFTERTHOUGHTS

I hope you have enjoyed my little run through Churchill's Secret Armies. I never intended it to be an in-depth piece, as I mentioned in the introduction, specialist books have told each glistening facet far better and in further depth than I.

I hope, however, hope to have blown the cobwebs off some obscure and not-so-obscure fighting forces, and provided a (hopefully) fascinating look into the special forces, units, and departments formed by Churchill and his administration. Even if I have just provided a decent overview, or a prompt to do some further reading, then my job is done.

I raise a glass to Winston Churchill, the man who seldom could say he was completely sober.

Yours

Ian Hall

# THE SUGGESTED READING PILE

As I researched the book, I dipped into a few books for information, details, quotes, and such. For your information, or in case you want to read further, here's a  short list of some of the books I used...

ISBN 1-58579-014-1 *Invasion 1940* by Peter Fleming (1956)

ISBN 978-0850520026 *Gubbins and SOE* by Peter Wilkinson and Joan Bright Astley (1993)

ISBN 1 86064 779-0 *Foreign Fields; The Story of an SOE Operative* by Peter Wilkinson (1997)

ISBN 978-1862272422 *Dennis Wheatley: Churchill's Storyteller* by Craig Cabell (2005)

ISBN 0306821974 *Churchill: The Power of Words* by Martin Gilbert (2013)

ISBN 978-0345548634 *The Last Lion: Winston Spencer Churchill: Defender of the Realm*, by William Manchester & Paul Reid (2013)

illustrated

"ALL IN FIGHTING ILLUSTRATED
CHURCHILLS
SECRET ARMY ARMY

Ar. INSURANCE (COPYRIGHT

Printed in Great Britain
by Amazon

55203868R00116